FANDOM FOR US, BY US

POSTMILLENNIAL POP

General Editors: Karen Tongson and Henry Jenkins

Puro Arte: Filipinos on the Stages of Empire
Lucy Mae San Pablo Burns

Media Franchising: Creative License and Collaboration in the Culture Industries
Derek Johnson

Your Ad Here: The Cool Sell of Guerrilla Marketing
Michael Serazio

Looking for Leroy: Illegible Black Masculinities
Mark Anthony Neal

From Bombay to Bollywood: The Making of a Global Media Industry
Aswin Punathambekar

A Race So Different: Performance and Law in Asian America
Joshua Takano Chambers-Letson

Surveillance Cinema
Catherine Zimmer

Modernity's Ear: Listening to Race and Gender in World Music
Roshanak Kheshti

The New Mutants: Superheroes and the Radical Imagination of American Comics
Ramzi Fawaz

Restricted Access: Media, Disability, and the Politics of Participation
Elizabeth Ellcessor

The Sonic Color Line: Race and the Cultural Politics of Listening
Jennifer Lynn Stoever

Diversión: Play and Popular Culture in Cuban America
Albert Sergio Laguna

Open TV: Innovation beyond Hollywood and the Rise of Web Television
Aymar Jean Christian

Antisocial Media: Anxious Labor in the Digital Economy
Greg Goldberg

More Than Meets the Eye: Special Effects and the Fantastic Transmedia Franchise
Bob Rehak

Spreadable Media: Creating Value and Meaning in a Networked Culture
Henry Jenkins, Sam Ford, and Joshua Green

Playing to the Crowd: Musicians, Audiences, and the Intimate Work of Connection
Nancy K. Baym

Old Futures: Speculative Fiction and Queer Possibility
Alexis Lothian

Anti-Fandom: Dislike and Hate in the Digital Age
Edited by Melissa A. Click

Social Media Entertainment: The New Intersection of Hollywood and Silicon Valley
Stuart Cunningham and David Craig

Video Games Have Always Been Queer
Bo Ruberg

The Power of Sports: Media and Spectacle in American Culture
Michael Serazio

The Race Card: From Gaming Technologies to Model Minorities
Tara Fickle

Open World Empire: Race, Erotics, and the Global Rise of Video Games
Christopher B. Patterson

The Content of Our Caricature: African American Comic Art and Political Belonging
Rebecca Wanzo

Stories of the Self: Life Writing after the Book
Anna Poletti

The Dark Fantastic: Race and the Imagination from Harry Potter to the Hunger Games
Ebony Elizabeth Thomas

Hip Hop Heresies: Queer Aesthetics in New York City
Shanté Paradigm Smalls

Digital Masquerade: Feminist Rights and Queer Media in China
Jia Tan

The Revolution Will Be Hilarious: Comedy for Social Change and Civic Power
Caty Borum

The Privilege of Play: A History of Hobby Games, Race, and Geek Culture
Aaron Trammell

Unbelonging: Inauthentic Sounds in Mexican and Latinx Aesthetics
Iván A. Ramos

Sonic Sovereignty: Hip Hop, Indigeneity, and Shifiting Popular Music Mainstreams
Liz Przybylski

Style: A Queer Cosmology
Taylor Black

Normporn: Queer Viewers and the TV That Soothes Us
Karen Tongson

Where the Wild Things Were: Boyhood and Permissive Parenting in Postwar America
Henry Jenkins

Fandom for Us, by Us: The Pleasures and Practices of Black Audiences
Alfred L. Martin, Jr.

Fandom for Us, by Us

*The Pleasures and Practices
of Black Audiences*

Alfred L. Martin, Jr.

NEW YORK UNIVERSITY PRESS
New York

NEW YORK UNIVERSITY PRESS
New York
www.nyupress.org

© 2025 by New York University
All rights reserved

Please contact the Library of Congress for Cataloging-in-Publication data.

ISBN: 9781479824908 (hardback)
ISBN: 9781479824922 (paperback)
ISBN: 9781479824946 (library ebook)
ISBN: 9781479824939 (consumer ebook)

This book is printed on acid-free paper, and its binding materials are chosen for strength and durability. We strive to use environmentally responsible suppliers and materials to the greatest extent possible in publishing our books.

Manufactured in the United States of America

10 9 8 7 6 5 4 3 2 1

Also available as an ebook

CONTENTS

Introduction: Fandom: Now in Black!   1

1. Class: Misty Copeland, Distinction, and Black Fandom   21

2. Clout: *Black Panther*, Doing It for the Culture, and Black Fandom   57

3. Canon: *The Wiz*, Interpretive Communities, and Black Fandom   95

4. Comfort: *The Golden Girls*, Resonance, and Black Fandom   127

Conclusion: Fandom for Us   161

Appendix: Interview Questions   169

Acknowledgments   173

Notes   177

Index   189

About the Author   191

Introduction

Fandom: Now in Black!

In August 1984, my mother took me and my sister Trena to see The Jacksons' Victory Tour at the Pontiac Silverdome in suburban Detroit. That woman stood in line and got us main floor, third row center seats, God bless her! At the concert, dressed in my replica "Beat It" jacket, I screamed myself hoarse (and it is truly the only time I remember leaving a concert venue with my ears still ringing for hours afterward). In addition to my replica "Beat It" jacket, I also had a replica "Billie Jean" jacket, I learned all the dance moves for "Thriller," and I knew all the words to every song on the *Thriller* album (including the few not released as singles). Yet, in my mind, I was not a fan. I am uncertain if my "failure" to understand myself as a Michael Jackson fan was the result of how the category "fan" is culturally and industrially constructed as white by default (and often male). Surely, I did not know about the white construction of "fan" as a nine-year-old. But perhaps, I felt it. After all, the mediated images of fandom I recall seeing as a child mostly involved shrieking white girls fainting at the sight of Elvis Presley and The Beatles through newsreel footage. That was not how my fandom manifested itself—at least not the fainting part (and even if I fainted, it would not be because of Elvis or The Beatles). It is not just that I did not feel "seen" within the category fan. But it was that, in some ways, my Michael Jackson fandom was different from what is often depicted and theorized as fandom.

My childhood Michael Jackson fandom is useful for thinking through the fandom-based concerns that animate *Fandom for Us, by Us*. The Victory Tour (and my flattening of it as a Michael Jackson concert) was one of the few music concerts my sisters and I went to where my mother accompanied us. Our family certainly saw other concerts and cultural events. I remember seeing early hip hop shows that included several acts on the same ticket: Run-DMC, Salt-N-Pepa, Kurtis Blow, and other pioneers. But my parents did not accompany us to those shows; it was just I and my sisters who attended. Jackson was, thus, elevated as belonging to a taste culture that could connect generations of Black folks. And in fact, in a recent conversation with my mother about the concert, she said she took us because she loved The Jacksons and we were her "pawns" to get to see them live. Thus, Michael and The Jacksons held a special place for my Black family such that my parents spent our limited capital (we were a lower middle-class family with four children, plus both parents) on tickets. But, in my mother's configuration of Jackson, he was important for passing down Black cultural heritage such that a "pilgrimage" to see him perform live was necessary—even if we were her "pawns." Attending The Jacksons' concert was important because as not just a global superstar, but a *Black* global superstar, it was imperative that Black folks support Michael. Jackson allowed my mother to simultaneously draw on Black nostalgia for The Jackson 5 and their "classic" catalog of music *and* build a fandom future with two of her children through Jackson's contemporary music. My reengagement with my Jackson fandom shaped how I began to think about Black fandom for *Fandom for Us, by Us*. Through Jackson, I began to think about the ways Black fandom draws on making *classed* distinctions between one fan object and another. I thought about Black fandom's engagement with consumer activism to flex the *clout* of Black audiences, viewers, and fans, to support "good," "family-friendly" Black content. I began to believe that Black fandom might create a Black archive that *canonizes* particular fan objects. And lastly, I hypothesized that Black fandom draws from ideals around nostalgia and the connection of generations of Black fans through the *comfort* of the object.

Fandom for Us, by Us springs from these observations, which resulted in the four C's of Black fandom that structure this book: *class, clout, canon,* and *comfort*. In that way, the theorization is "mine." But the four C's of Black fandom are a grounded theory, which means that while I certainly had hypotheses about how Black fandom worked, the *actual* theory comes from the Black fans who lent their voices to this project. I did not "impose" the four C's of Black fandom on their interview data, but rather, I allowed the four C's to emerge from what they revealed about the ways Black folks engage with fan objects. In short, the nearly

70 Black fans whose voices shifted and sharpened how I understood Black fandom are the backbone of *Fandom for Us, by Us*.

Black folks are interested in media because of the meanings they extract from it and the ways Black life can be mapped onto those images. They engage with images to distinguish "good" from "less good/bad" (class). They consume media to demonstrate the kinds of images they hope mainstream media industries will produce (clout). Black folks choose images because they are important "for the culture" (canon). And they turn to certain images because they are relaxing (comfort). In short, these four C's—(1) class, (2) clout, (3) canon, and (4) comfort—are the organizing logics of Black fandom, which I will discuss in more detail later in this introduction. But ultimately, this grounded theory dwells in the gray area between representation and reception.

From Representation to Reception

Representation matters. That has become a mantra for those invested in images and image production. However, mediated Black representation has always been mired in a feedback loop trying to get representation "right" because it presumably matters. On television, *Beulah* (CBS, 1950–1953) and *Amos 'n Andy* (CBS, 1951–1953) were too closely tethered to historical Black stereotypes like the Mammy and the Sambo, resulting in the National Association for the Advancement of Colored People (NAACP) leading a boycott against *Amos 'n Andy* to get the program removed from airwaves. When *Julia* (NBC, 1966–1968) debuted, the lead character was understood in some circles as not Black enough or what series star Diahann Carroll later described as "a white negro," a character removed from the experiences of ordinary Black people in a post–Civil Rights America.[1] Black-cast sitcoms of the 1970s like *Good Times* (CBS, 1974–1979) attempted to answer the call to make Blackness on television more "real" and less tethered to an imaginary fantasy world where racial harmony was the order of the day, like in *Julia*. *Good Times*, set in Chicago's Cabrini Green housing project, turned to relevant topics like race and class to reflect the struggles Black Americans were still experiencing in the wake of the alleged realization of Dr. Martin Luther King, Jr.'s "dream." But, like *Amos 'n Andy*, *Good Times* was "too real" and too closely associated with Black stereotypes, particularly J.J. Evans as portrayed by Jimmie Walker. Media scholar Adrien Sebro details how series stars Esther Rolle and John Amos resented how J.J. was fashioned as a buffoonish stereotype of Blackness.[2] The 1980s saw the rise of *The Cosby Show* (NBC, 1984–1992) which attempted to avoid the stereotypes presented in *Amos 'n Andy*. Representationally, *The Cosby Show* kept the class positionality of *Julia* and the nuclear family from *Good Times*. Yet even that was criticized for being "too white" and not "real" enough, even as the work of Black visual artists and clothing representing historically Black colleges and universities were omnipresent within the series. On the one hand, as media and cultural studies scholars Sut Jhally and Justin Lewis revealed, Black *Cosby Show* viewers deemed the series a necessary fiction to "fix" how white folks thought about real Black folks.[3] On the other hand, many white folks in Jhally and Lewis's study, aided by the conservative politics of Ronald Reagan's administration, demonized Black communities for not adequately picking themselves up by their bootstraps as the fictional Huxtables had. And while the Huxtables were not Black enough in the 1980s, the 1990s saw series like *In Living Color* (Fox, 1990–1994) and *Martin* (Fox, 1992–1997) trade on the popularity of hip hop's sounds and style, though they, too, were often deemed "too Black." And the feedback loop continues . . .

In short, while representation might matter, it can never get it "right" for at least three reasons. First, representation is simulacrum, and if, as sociologist Jean Baudrillard suggests, simulacrum is a copy of a copy of a copy of a copy of a copy of the real, then representation can never be unquestionably "real" or "authentic."[4] Second, and related, what makes representation "real" or "authentic" is the act of reception. In other words, it is not necessarily that representation matters, as much as there is an invisible "to me" behind the phrase. Representation is personal. Representation is felt. Representation makes one feel seen. Representation resonates. Third, Black representation, as taken up by Black people, is often mired in a double consciousness such that it is partly judged on how others (especially white viewers) will make meaning from texts. In this way, representation is not simply felt or personal; rather, representation is evaluated by how the "other" decodes it.[5] Taken together, I argue that reception is central to understanding representation. In *Fandom for Us, by Us*, I am interested in how representation resonates for Black audiences and fans. In particular, I explore how and when Black resonances are contingent on a mainstream idea(l). The concerns of *Fandom for Us, by Us* are twofold: first, it centers how representation resonates for Black fans; second, it investigates the ways whiteness and white institutions structure Black representation. This juncture undergirds Black fandom's relationship to class, clout, canon, and comfort.

Examining Fandom for Us, by Us

Nearly 25 years into the 21st century, there remain few studies that examine Black reception practices. I am declaring the time has finally come to holistically study Black fan practices. But even as I center Black fans' practices and voices in *Fandom for Us, by Us*, I simultaneously assert both the particularity of Black fandom and its universality. To explain what I mean by the particularity of Blackness and its universality, I want to use the image of one's hand. *Fandom for Us, by Us* is about the specific languages, gestures, and cultural literacies of Blackness. These practices metaphorically represent the literal Black side of the hand, or the side of the hand with melanin. Simultaneously, the "other" side looks similar on most people's hands. This speaks to the metaphorical ways some Black fannish practices are universal and shared across racial categories (including whiteness). Thus, while *Fandom for Us, by Us* forcefully centers the study of Blackness and Black fandom, it also asserts that "unraced" fandom as well as the fandom of other communities of color can learn from the contours of Black reception practices. Thus, Black fandom is both universal *and* particular.

Throughout this book, I use the term "Black fandom" because it adequately captures what is under study within the project. It is not just how Black folks watch a text or set of texts, but how and why they interpret texts and make meaning from them. At the same time, I want to acknowledge that Black fandom is not monolithic (just as Blackness itself is not monolithic). Certainly, the work in *Fandom for Us, by Us* is extrapolatable across Black fandoms, but it is not my claim that I am uncovering universal "Black fandom" (as if such a thing were possible). Rather, like anthropologist Clifford Geertz articulated in his work, my goal is to not generalize Black fandom writ large, but to generalize within the specific Black fandoms I study.[6] Further, within the pages of *Fandom for Us, by Us*, I am less interested in analyzing Black culture than in trying to understand how Black fans understand what they do with fan objects.

Fandom for Us, by Us is also about Black cultural politics. That is, the book engages how the visual functions as the terrain on which Black fans struggle over meaning. And while the feminist mantra that "the personal is political" is true, the visual is also political for Black fans, because, for them, representation matters. If media makes Black people "feel seen" and acknowledged, then media negotiates questions about what it means to be Black; what it means to feel part of the United States of America and part of a Black culture; what inclusion and exclusion from media discourse feels like; and how the empty signifier that is mediated Blackness is filled up with meaning. In other words, Blackness is not made *in* media, but is partly constituted *through* media, centering the importance of reception and fannish practices. In sum, reception and fannish practices are central to understanding Black media images. Black cultural politics animate how Black fans engage media. The very act of media consumption is not always configured as centrally pleasurable. Rather, Black consumption practices are often set against the context of industrial logics. The act of Black looking is not just about the look. The Black look fashions meaning within the logics of media production. The Black look is used to "show Hollywood" the viability of Black audiences. The logic goes that if Black folks go to the opera house to see Misty Copeland dance, or to the movie theater to watch *Black Panther* or *The Wiz*, or stream/otherwise watch *The Golden Girls*, then there will be more Black ballet stars and production of films and television programs that feature Black talent and cater to Black audiences.

While Black fandom is certainly central, my training as a media and cultural studies scholar means that *Fandom for Us, by Us* is informed by the circuit of media study. As feminist media scholar Julie D'Acci suggests about the circuit of media study, each node marks "out a convergence of discursive practices, which as the phrase indicates are themselves convergences of meaning and matter (including people, environments, and money)."[7] Put simply, while *Fandom for Us, by Us* is about Black fan practices, it is equally about representation, media industries, and specific cultural epochs that inform those fandoms. Of particular interest in D'Acci's circuit of media study is her placement of the researcher within the circuit because, as she notes, "it is the researcher [. . .] who produces his or her versions of the object and the articulations."[8] I am, unquestionably, the ringmaster of *Fandom for Us, by Us*, and as such, I do not want to attempt to hide behind some semblance of scholarly objectivity.

Fandom for Us, by Us is driven not necessarily by a desire to understand how Black folks do fandom; rather I am interested in *why* Black folks do fandom. Asking *how* fandom functions engenders a description of practices that can easily become tethered to the particularities of a case study. Asking *why* Black fandom operates as it does requires a description of fannish behaviors, but it simultaneously requires a discussion of what Black fans gain from their fan objects. My aim is to get closer to being able to answer why Black fans interact with their fan objects. In coming to a particular fan object, why do Black fans engage class, clout, canon, and comfort?

Building a Black Bridge: Black Reception and Fandom Studies

Fandom for Us, by Us is conceptualized as what television producer Mara Brock-Akil calls "Black on purpose." Film and media studies scholar Kristen Warner describes "Black on purpose" as related to a cultural specificity in which "all the experiences, histories, and cultures that are tied" to Blackness are on full display.[9] In making this book "Black on purpose," I also shift the terrain on which its claims rest. I am uninterested in fighting for the recognition of Blackness within fan studies writ large because, as novelist Toni Morrison said about the work of racism: it wants to distract so that you do the work of proving the importance of the work instead of actually doing the work.[10] Race generally, and Blackness specifically, can easily be sidestepped by asking folks to answer a question they never considered before they can answer the one on which they want to work. As such, *Fandom for Us, by Us* takes up cultural theorists Isaac Julien and Kobena Mercer's call for "the potential break-up or deconstruction of structures that determine what is regarded as culturally central and what is regarded as culturally marginal."[11] *Fandom for Us, by Us* does not ask for a seat at white fandom's table; rather, it makes a table for Black fandom that is, as Solange sings in her song "F.U.B.U.," "for us, this shit is for us." In other words, in *Fandom for Us, by Us*, I do not spend time attempting to convince whiteness that Black fandom is worthy of study. Instead, I just do the work of studying Black fandom. Nor do I treat Black fandom as aberrant by comparing it to more "normative" white fan practices. Sometimes Black fan practices converge with white fan practices as much as they diverge. And that is okay. The work I undertake in *Fandom for Us, by Us* treats Black fandom as a complex and varied set of practices that engages with class, clout, canon, and comfort, and builds on the work of key Black thinkers around Blackness and reception and fan practices.

Fandom for Us, by Us builds on and is indebted to the work of communication scholar Robin Means Coleman, feminist scholar Jacqueline Bobo, feminist scholar Rebecca Wanzo, film and media scholar Kristen Warner, and media studies scholar Beretta Smith Shomade, whose work on Black audiences and Black fandoms has been foundational. Means Coleman's and Bobo's work is seminal for its attention to Black audiences through in-depth interviews. Means Coleman suggests that studying how Black folks "engage with dominant cultural forms, work to make sense of their own conditions, and consider the convergence of these conditions with the represented worlds of media" is a crucial front for media and cultural studies.[12] Similarly, Bobo argues for the activeness of Black audiences and fans who use the meanings they construct from media texts "to empower themselves and their social group."[13] Important in Bobo's work is her engagement with the activeness of Black audiences to use media as a tool for the improvement of the whole of Black culture. Taken together, Means Coleman and Bobo make a compelling case for studying the meaning-making practices of Black folks not in the abstract, but by engaging with the real, living, breathing, and embodied experiences of Black folks. They also collectively illuminate that studying Black audiences should go beyond understanding what Black folks do with media, to understanding why they engage with media.

Wanzo and Warner build on Bobo's and Means Coleman's foundational work to move from discussions of Black audiences to Black fans and fandom practices. Wanzo suggests that fandom's continued disciplinary elision of race generally, and Blackness in particular, is likely "because [Blackness] troubles some of the claims—and desires—at the heart of fan studies scholars and their scholarship."[14] Warner adds that Black fandom often "exists as its own niche area" because Black folks "choose to exist despite their invisibility and exclusion from mainstream fan spaces. Further, exclusion pushed them to develop spaces where their own interests, agendas, and perspectives could be foregrounded."[15] Warner forwards that Black fans do not necessarily bemoan their exclusion from "general" fandom, but Black fans find and make spaces where they can do fandom where, how, and why they please. While working in the realm of the theoretical rather than necessarily with "real" fans (although Warner engages with Twitter discourse), both Wanzo and Warner laid important groundwork for centering Blackness within fan studies *and* thinking through how Black fandoms are simultaneously universal and particular.

Recognizing the fully active and intelligent nature of Black viewers and fans, Smith Shomade's and Brown's work is important to understand the interplay between Black audiences/fans and media industries. Smith Shomade thinks through how BET commodified Black audiences and how those Black audiences responded to the content the network mediated, especially its music videos featuring Black women.[16] Continuing this work of understanding the interplay between Black fans and media industries, Brown argues that:

> interpretation is a complex process shaped by inter- and intra-textual information shared with, and about, other fans and the creators themselves. [. . .] Popular texts [. . . are] interpreted according to the ideological encodings of the producers and the socially positioned, fandom-based, decodings of the audience. [. . .] In other words, there is a sort of "contract" of meaning that exists between the two sides and positions any interpretation of textual ideology as both a personal and mutual concept.[17]

Smith Shomade centers what I have elsewhere argued is Black fandom's intertwining of economic consumption, Pavlovian responses to Black representation, and "attentiveness to the machinations of the culture industries."[18] In sum, then, Black fan practices are not "just" about reception. They are equally embedded in representational/textual practices, industrial practices, and sociocultural contexts. These concerns undergird my exploration of Black fan practices through class, clout, canon, and comfort in *Fandom for Us, by Us*.

Studying Black Fans

I want to be clear that, in *Fandom for Us, by Us*, I am not attempting to (re)pathologize fans—especially Black fans—by investigating why they are fans of certain media and celebrities. Instead, I want to magnify these Black fans' voices by highlighting what they like and why they like. In so doing, I hope to illuminate the productivity of Black fan labor in both its joy and its pain. Here I partly invoke the song by R&B group Frankie Beverly & Maze "Joy and Pain," in which they assert that "joy and pain are like sunshine and rain" or different sides of the same coin. Joy is, in many ways, an analytic through which much of fandom/fandom studies is often discussed. But I want to center the *Black* joy Black folks derive from Misty Copeland, *Black Panther, The Wiz,* and *The Golden Girls*. Seeing Copeland's Black body where they have not seen bodies that look like hers (or theirs) invokes joy. Seeing a major Hollywood studio invest in a fantastical Black-cast film like *Black Panther* brings Black folks joy in the present and hope for the future. Repeatedly engaging with and "mastering" *The Wiz* is joyful. Black folks find joy in watching the antics of four old white ladies as they share a home together in Miami in *The Golden Girls*.

But Black fandom can also be painful. My invocation of pain does not suggest that Black fandom causes distress with respect to these fan objects, but instead invokes *pain* as a verb to suggest that Black fandoms involve effort taken to accomplish something. Black folks use their money to support Blackness via Misty Copeland and *Black Panther* in the hope that their capital will result in industrial change: more Black ballerinas and more high-budget Black-cast films. Black fandoms labor to canonize *The Wiz* and center specific Black cultural tastes. Black fans labor to read *The Golden Girls* Blackly to make it resonate. Thus, the "pain" associated with Black fandoms is a political fandom rooted in a way to make media resonate and center Black cultural competencies.

Fandom for Us, by Us is similarly bound within my own feminism in which the personal and the political are inextricably linked. It is personal in its centering of Blackness. As I stated in previous work, while I am a Black gay man, I lead with and center my Blackness because, when I walk into any room or situation, "my Blackness and maleness are the clues someone encountering me for the first time uses to read my body. My gayness might not be detectable until I speak or stand a certain way or perform a certain act."[19] Additionally, my subject position as a Black person and scholar enmeshes me in the subject matter of the book, making the work I undertake personal. As a former ballet dancer, that personal history cannot be extracted from a study of the world's most famous Black ballerina. As a Black fan of *The Golden Girls* and *The Wiz*, I am both apart from the other Black fans I study, because I am a researcher, and a part of the Black fan tribe. With *The Golden Girls*, I was truly fascinated that there were other Black fans of the series because the category "*Golden Girls* fan" is configured within popular culture as white and/or gay. As a Black person attuned to the machinations of media industries with respect to Blackness, I cannot be completely extracted from the hopes and dreams some Black *Black Panther* and *The Wiz* fans placed on the films and what they might mean for the future of Black-cast film production. Thus, as a Black gay researcher, I am what sociologist Patricia Hill Collins calls an "outsider within"—one who is simultaneously part of a group and apart from it.[20] At the same time, I position myself within a lineage of Black scholar/fans who Wanzo posits have "intimate knowledge" about Black communities "that has often been essential in fields where Black histories have not been addressed."[21]

The personal intersects with the political in the citational politics I employ in *Fandom for Us, by Us*. First and foremost, *Fandom for Us, by Us* is interested in building on Wanzo's work by continuing to draw a Black genealogy of fandom/fan practices by signal-boosting the work of scholars working on Blackness, Black audiences, and Black fan practices. This book is specifically about signal-boosting Black scholars' work. *Fandom for Us, by Us* is, thus, a love letter to Blackness: Black people, Black scholars, Black work, and Black fandom. And even as the work I undertake in *Fandom for Us, by Us* is Black, it still asks, as artist Arthur Jafa did: "How come we can't be as Black as we are and still be universal?"[22] In other words, *Fandom for Us, by Us* offers that Black fan practices are both specific to Blackness and can help to illuminate how other races of people (including white people) do fandom.

A Word on Method

Methodologically, *Fandom for Us, by Us* principally uses in-depth interviews with Black fans of Misty Copeland, *Black Panther*, *The Wiz*, and *The Golden Girls*. I also use online data from spaces like Facebook, Instagram, TikTok, and Twitter to help elucidate how Black folks do fandom.[23] My interviews principally work to answer why Black folks do fandom as they do and to complicate a unified, essentialized Black fandom that manifests in a range of practices.

I am certain that as a Black scholar studying Black fan practices, Black folks were more willing to hear my pitch for research participants. And once they were open to participating in my research, our shared racial and cultural identity shaped our conversations. After all, as Sut Jhally and Justin Lewis explain about their work, "to ease the discomfort people might feel in addressing [race . . .] Black groups [were interviewed] by Black interviewers, a strategy that was clearly validated when we analyzed the transcripts."[24] So, whether it was my Black body approaching Black patrons at ABT performances where Misty Copeland was slated to dance or my Black avatar on Twitter asking Black folks to talk about *Black Panther* or *The Golden Girls*, my Blackness likely made the ask easier and the responses, presumably, less guarded, mediated, and restrained.

But I would be remiss if I did not note that, in attempting to create a bond with participants that would elicit "better" interview data, I often code-switched between "proper" and vernacular forms of English—specifically African American Vernacular English (AAVE). While I certainly used the interview script/questions (see the appendix) approved by the Institutional Review Board (IRB), the questions during the interviews often followed the spirit of the question rather than how they were written for approval. For example, instead of asking "How did you first hear about Misty Copeland?" I instead asked, "How did you find out Misty Copeland was a thing?" The colloquial nature of the ask (with attendant inflection) is part of how I demonstrated that while I am a researcher attempting to glean information from interviewees, I am also similar to the interviewees' subject positions.

Part of the "problem" in doing the work I undertake within *Fandom for Us, by Us* is that interviewees could be telling me what they think I want to hear or are outright lying to me about their fan engagement. In employing AAVE and more casual language, I attempted to be understood as more of an "insider" than a "outsider" doing research and, thus, to get closer to a truth from these Black fans. Regardless of what these Black fans told me during our interviews, I assumed they were engaging with me in good faith and telling me *their* truth, which is informed by discourse, their own subject position, and perhaps even by the act of being "studied." The stories these Black fans told me ultimately reveal how Black fan practices are not simply informed by their fan object, but by discourse around and about their fan objects as well.

The Black people whose words I use as the primary data throughout *Fandom for Us, by Us* were recruited in several ways (recruitment details are provided in the individual chapters). Many of the interviewees were recruited via the social media networks Facebook and Twitter. Inherent in this recruitment strategy is a particular social situation of interviewees: they are social media literate, and because I used my own social media accounts to begin the recruitment, they are situated similarly to my own situation: they are mostly middle-class and mostly formally educated. To find Black Misty Copeland and some *Golden Girls* fans, I went to events to recruit: performances at which Misty Copeland was performing and *Golden Girls*–themed pop-up restaurants in New York and Chicago. To put it another way, while many of the interviewees were relatively "convenient" to find, for those that were not, I went to the places where I could find them. On the one hand, I should be clear that I had institutional support that allowed me to travel to find these harder-to-reach Black fans. On the other hand, because their voices were too important to rest on simply being unable to find them in the ways most convenient for me, I likely would have used my own money to amplify these Black voices.

Fandom for Us, by Us is also undergirded by my own politics around studying Black audiences. Within three of the four chapters, I provide sidebars that introduce the Black fans whose voices help in the theorization of the four C's of Black fandom. I do this to ensure, as much as possible, that these Black folks do not appear as data points whose individual knowledges were extracted for my scholarly gain. To that end, I use each participant's real first name rather than a pseudonym. In short, I want these Black fans to be seen as real people because their voices are integral to the grounded theory that has made *Fandom for Us, by Us* possible. I could have placed these Black fan snapshots in an appendix, but to my mind, that feels like putting them at the back of the proverbial bus—and I want to ensure that Blackness and Black people are as front and center as possible throughout this book. My hope is that in providing these snapshots that *Fandom for Us, by Us* readers can connect with these Black fans in some way. And that the Black fans who lent me their voices know that they are appreciated and that this book would be impossible without them.

The Four Chapters and C's of Black Fandom

Fandom for Us, by Us is organized around the four C's of Black fandom: class, clout, canon, and comfort. To demonstrate the four C's, I use four Black fandom fan objects: the Black ballerina Misty Copeland (*class*), the Black-led blockbuster *Black Panther* (2018, dir. Ryan Coogler) (*clout*), the Black-cast blockbuster *The Wiz* (1978, dir. Sidney Lumet) (*canon*), and the white-cast sitcom *The Golden Girls* (NBC, 1985–1992) (*comfort*). While each chapter centers a "C" and an attendant fandom object that helps illuminate its innerworkings, the four C's of Black fandom are not mutually exclusive; rather, each "C" reinforces and revises the others en route to an understanding of Black fan practices. That is, class is not separated from clout in a discussion of the way Black fans take up Misty Copeland and *Black Panther*. The Black fan choice of *The Wiz*, for example, is as classed as Misty Copeland and *Black Panther* as it is canonized. And *The Golden Girls* is similarly classed and canonized while providing Black fans comfort.

Chapter 1 uses Misty Copeland to demonstrate the intersection of Black fan practices and *class*. On June 30, 2015, Copeland, a member of American Ballet Theatre (ABT) since 2001, was promoted to the rank of principal dancer—the first Black woman to achieve the rank with the company in its then 75-year history. Like Barack Obama's 2008 election as America's first Black president, with her promotion, Copeland became a symbol of racial progress and the possibilities for Blackness within the typically lily-white world of ballet. Aside from being a fascinating media figure, Copeland helps to illuminate how Blackness, visibility, and "high" art converge in Black fan practices. I do not suggest that the idea of

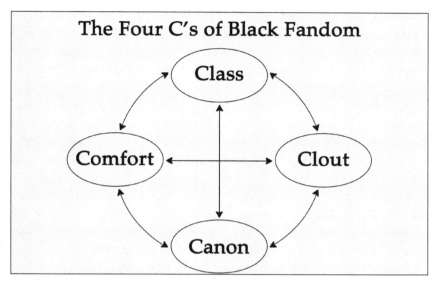

Figure 1.1. The four C's of Black fandom are not separate practices, but are practices that reinforce and build on one another. © Taylor Cole Miller. Photo used with permission.

"highbrow" has any currency per se—particularly because of the racist ways the term has been utilized within cultural practices and productions. Rather, placing Copeland within this designation simply suggests that ballet, as a highbrow art form, "tends to be associated with specific social contexts, those that are relatively inaccessible to the average person."[25] Put another way, Copeland allows me to explore why her fandom is contingent on a *classed* distinction between white, nationally recognized ballet companies and multicultural and/or regional ballet companies. Copeland as "high" art also allows for an examination of the ways Black fans understand and embrace her Black body in an artform with which they have little familiarity.

Class, then, as a Black fan practice, not only references socioeconomic status but is also concerned with Black taste cultures. Building on what Patricia A. Banks calls *Black cultivated consumption*, I use Copeland to work through how Black folks' fandom is "rooted in a desire to respond to and rectify legacies of Black marginality as well as continuing Black inequality."[26] For Black fans, because they have not previously known of the existence of Black dancers in ballet companies—an artform rightly understood as blindingly white—Copeland represents a break into a space that has historically been less than welcoming to Black folks. I also deploy *class* to center how it is not just Copeland's position within *any* ballet company, or one with primarily white dancers, but her status as a principal dancer with *American Ballet Theatre* that activates the classed distinctions Black fans make when taking her up as a fan object. As Tameka, who will be introduced more fully in chapter 1, says about Copeland's position in ABT, "American Ballet Theatre . . . like they're the number one and then you go down to the other ballet companies? Is that how it works?" While that is not "how it works," the fact is that, like consumer brands, the "American" in ABT's name is imbued with value for Copeland's Black fans. Thus, in *Fandom for Us, by Us, class* is not just about the fandoms Black folks enjoy, but about how the politics of particular kinds of visibility are associated with those fandoms.

Black Panther, with its $200 million budget, represented the first time since 1978 that a major Hollywood studio chose to greenlight a big-budget Black-cast film. There had certainly been "important" Black films in the ensuing 40 years: among them, *The Color Purple* (1985, dir. Steven Spielberg), *Malcolm X* (1992, dir. Spike Lee), *What's Love Got to Do with It* (1993, dir. Brian Gibson), and *Dreamgirls* (2006, dir. Bill Condon). Adjusted for 2018 dollars, those films' budgets were $42 million for *The Wiz*, $35 million for *The Color Purple*, $60 million for *Malcolm X*, $26 million for *What's Love Got to Do with It*, and $87 million for *Dreamgirls*. In short, no Black-cast film had come close to *Black Panther*'s production budget, and for Black folks, that meant something for its attendant fandom. In chapter 2, I use the film to explore what I have described elsewhere as "must-see Blackness," or Black fans' feeling of "'civic duty' to see Blackness in all of its forms."[27] In other words, *Black Panther* is useful to examine how Blackness, visibility, and consumer citizenship intersect within Black fan practices. Or, to put it plainly, how and why do Black folks exercise *clout* to support specific Black-cast media productions?

Clout, as a Black fandom practice, refers to Black fans' realization of Black consumer spending power as an agent for industrial change. In 2011, the Nielsen company released its first report detailing the spending power of Black consumers to "raise awareness of the economic clout [they] yielded."[28] In chapter 2, I explore how Black folks'

Black Panther fandom was principally rooted in the political mobilization of the Black look. The logic of *clout* suggests that Black fans use their consumer spending power, that is, the act of looking, to not only demonstrate their viability as a consumer segment, but to satiate and signal-boost their hunger for specific kinds of media content. As Channon, who will be introduced in chapter 2, says, "My husband and I actually talked about it. We really wanted to [see *Black Panther*] on the box office weekend, like on the first weekend [. . .]. It's not the first time we've intentionally tried to see something on the opening weekend just to contribute to the numbers." As Channon details, Black clout is driven by a politics of visibility with respect to Blackness on screen, Blackness vis-à-vis media industries, and Blackness as consumer citizenship.

Whereas the longer legacy of *Black Panther* has yet to fully be determined, chapter 3 explores the Black-cast film musical *The Wiz*'s importance to/for Black communities in the nearly 50 years since its theatrical release. In graduate school, I discovered that *The Wiz* did not recoup its production budget and was, as such, understood as a failure that put the final nail in the coffin of Black-cast film production in the late 1970s following the successful run earlier in the decade of Black-cast films pejoratively dubbed Blaxploitation by members of the Hollywood chapter of the NAACP. Christopher Sieving argued that *The Wiz*'s $23.4 million budget "ensured . . . severe losses when [it] opened to small audiences."[29] While *The Wiz*, indeed, did not recoup its production budget in its original theatrical run, the film did not open "to small audiences" as much as it opened to small *white* audiences. For example, at New York's Loews Astor Plaza, *The Wiz* broke office records primarily because, as *Variety* writer Frank Segers points out, most of the audience was Black.[30] As such, while *The Wiz* continues to circulate broadly, it mostly circulates within whiteness as a cult film, but in Black communities as a canonical one, particularly for Black baby boomers and Gen Xers. Rather than cede the center to white taste cultures and study *The Wiz* as a cult film, I use canon to allow Black taste to take up space as important and central. And in that centering, *The Wiz* affords asking: why and how do Black fan communities *canonize* Black media production?

Canon formation is bound within specific taste cultures; as Rhea, one of the members of a friend group called the Potluck Crew (of which I am also a member), details, she introduced her friends' children to *The

Wiz. She told them, "'We need to watch *The Wiz*.' And one of the kids asked, 'What is it with this?' Then after the first viewing, she said, 'Let's watch it again!' And now every Friday this group of kids are watching *The Wiz*. It's just stuff like that keeps me coming back [to *The Wiz*] regularly." Rhea's comments help shape chapter 3's theorization of *canon* as a communal reception/fannish practice that rests on at least four criteria. First, Black canon is necessarily unconcerned with how a film looks or is put together. Second, and related, something designated as within the Black canon centers Black feeling and affect as a reception response over aesthetic valuations. Third, a Black canon object is shared intergenerationally. Fourth, the canonized object takes on meaning outside of its original context and is, perhaps, used among groups of friends or family as a shorthand language.

The Golden Girls is a television series about four white ladies (Bea Arthur's Dorothy Zbornak, Betty White's Rose Nylund, Rue McClanahan's Blanche Devereaux, and Estelle Getty's Sophia Petrillo) who share a home together in Miami. Although the series infrequently featured Black characters, through the flow of its original Saturday night broadcast, where it was programmed alongside Black-cast series like *227* (NBC, 1985–1990) and *Amen* (NBC, 1985–1991), it was consumed by some Black viewers (myself included). Because of this general Black representational absence, *The Golden Girls* allows an examination of Black fandom divorced from Black representation. In short, chapter 4 asks how *comfort* intersects with Black fandom to explore how joy is a Black fannish practice.

Comfort, as a Black fandom practice, is concerned with the nostalgic and sentimental affects associated with a beloved fan object. Partly, *comfort* is most directly connected to notions of Black joy. That is not to say *class*, *clout*, and *canon* are not joyous, but it is to suggest that *comfort* is about the moments when Black folks can just be themselves and let their proverbial hair down. Black *Golden Girls* fandom helps illuminate how Black *comfort* is deeply imbedded in the ways anxieties are eased and (re)assurances are provided. Alba, a Black *Golden Girls* fan who will be introduced in chapter 4, says that "as an adult [*The Golden Girls*] was comforting because, I think initially it reminded me of being a kid. And then eventually it just became . . . My mom used to say, 'Her girls are on.' And when that happened, she was not going to pay attention to you.'" It is no surprise that people find comfort in particular media texts. How Black *comfort* differs as a Black fandom practice is in its connection with ideas about family and home that are mapped onto *comforting* fan objects, like the white-cast series *The Golden Girls*.

Through class, clout, canon, and comfort, *Fandom for Us, by Us* examines how Black fandom for Misty Copeland, *Black Panther*, *The Wiz*, and *The Golden Girls* is imbricated in a messy and difficult to codify politics of representation. Taken together, the chapters in this book provide a portrait of the multivalent ways fandom works both for us and by us.

1

Class

Misty Copeland, Distinction, and Black Fandom

In her memoir, *Life in Motion: An Unlikely Ballerina*, Misty Copeland recounts a journal entry she wrote after declining an invitation to join Dance Theatre of Harlem (DTH), a ballet company founded by former New York City Ballet principal dancer Arthur Mitchell in 1969 to give Black ballet dancers an opportunity to professionally perform classical ballets. She wrote, "In contemplating Arthur's invitation, I had felt the full emotional force of how badly I wanted to succeed at ABT [American Ballet Theatre]. How I couldn't give up, couldn't run away, and if I had to work ten times harder than everyone else, then I would so I'd always know that I'd tried. I'd fought way too hard to abandon my dream of being a principal dancer with ABT. I wanted always to know that I'd stood my ground, whether or not I got my reward."[1] This excerpt from Copeland's memoir is a useful starting point for this chapter's exploration of class, as I deploy it in *Fandom for Us, by Us*. As a professional ballerina and as a human, Copeland is certainly allowed to have dreams with respect to where her career will take her. At the same time, she has endowed ABT with so much value that to succeed there presumably meant more. Or, as she writes later in her memoir, "it would be so much easier to be in a company where I stood out because of my gifts and not the color of my skin."[2] When presented with the choice to dance with DTH where her talent would be seen and celebrated in a sea of mostly brown ballerinas, she chose to fight to make a place for herself in a mostly white ballet company—even if it meant, as the adage goes, she had to work twice as hard to get half as much in ABT. And while the fight is admirable, particularly in an era where diversity, equity, and inclusion efforts have captured attention from classrooms and boardrooms to movie houses and opera houses, Copeland seemingly makes a distinction between the mostly Black DTH and the mostly white ABT, suggesting that one has more cultural cachet than the other.

This chapter is principally concerned with explicating how distinction, or what I deploy as *class*, functions as one of the four C's of Black fandom. Throughout this chapter, I deploy *class* in four overlapping and interconnected ways. First, class references socioeconomic status: two-thirds of the Black Misty Copeland fans I interviewed make more than $75,000 per year. For the purposes of the work in this chapter, higher socioeconomic status is connected to ballet in its classed privilege. For example, the cost of ballet class tuition and ballet attire alone is a costly endeavor. Serious dancers usually take classes five or more days per week, which often includes private lessons that, when I taught private ballet lessons, cost $50 per hour. For girls, there is the additional added cost of pointe shoes, which average about $100 per pair and last anywhere from a week to a month. A parent of a ballet student I formerly taught estimated that in one year she spent roughly $10,000 for her daughter's lessons, attire, pointe shoes, and performances. Thus, even as a hobby, let alone a potential career path, ballet assumes a certain class positionality.

Moving from the ballet barre to the theater as spectator, tickets to see live ballet performances are also expensive. Adding Copeland's celebrity into the mix makes it a still more expensive endeavor. For example, tickets to see Copeland perform Odette/Odile in *Swan Lake* at the Detroit Opera House in 2017 started at $125, whereas to see other ballerinas perform the same role, tickets could be procured for as little as $27 (these were, of course, seats near the back of the 2,700-seat venue). That is not to say that Black folks might not be fans of the ballet *Swan Lake* or ballet generally. But the cost of a ticket to see Copeland suggests many who paid the price of admission were Copeland fans. In short, seeing Copeland dance, presumably as a Copeland fan, adds cost to an already potentially costly night at the ballet. Thus, for her Black fans, seeing Copeland is not simply a "flex" of capital by paying the price of the ticket to see her; it is engaged with a classed politics of visibility that values seeing Copeland over other non-Black ballerinas as Odette/Odile.

I marry socioeconomic status with sociologist Cassi Pittman Clayton's assertion that "Black consumers who have cultural capital, credentials, and cash to spend" continue to "contend with the subtle and not

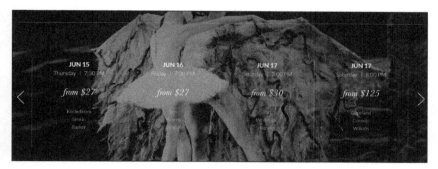

Figure 1.1. Image from Detroit Opera House website showing ticket prices for American Ballet Theatre performances of *Swan Lake*.

so subtle notions that Blacks are culturally and socially inferior."[3] Put another way, Black fans spend to show that they can, but also do so in the service of beloved objects and events—like seeing Misty Copeland. Black Copeland fandom is, thus, also enmeshed in #BlackExcellence. Her Black fans attempt to "signal-boost" Copeland as a Black woman excelling in a mostly white space. In so doing, Black fans practice what Pittman Clayton calls *Black cultivated consumption*—or using their Black dollars "to respond to and rectify legacies of Black marginality as well as continuing Black inequality."[4] Copeland's Black fans partly rally around her because Black folks have historically been unwelcomed within the Eurocentric ballet world.

Second, my deployment of class is rooted in sociologists Crystal Fleming and Lorraine Roses's assertion that Black cultural capitalists consume "high culture" Black objects to promote "'good' Black 'culture.'"[5] The distinctions between "good" and "bad" Black cultural production are certainly fraught and entangled in Black respectability politics, but they are useful for how Black fans engage with their fandom objects. For example, the middle-class Black women I interviewed for a project on Tyler Perry's anti-fandom have a vexed relationship to his media output. One of the Black women I interviewed for that project said, "In his films you get D-class actors, you get D-class everything. You get subpar everything . . . subpar location, subpar crew, subpar budget."[6] Without necessarily invoking the language of "good" and "bad" explicitly, this woman clearly articulates that, in her configuration of Perry as a creator, he is "D-class." As I will demonstrate throughout this chapter, Copeland is far from being designated as a "D-class" ballerina with respect to her fans. This classed distinction between "bad" and "good" is also demonstrated by the importance Black fans place on Copeland's position within ABT versus another ballet company. The fannish choice of Copeland is classed in the ways it positions her as suitable to be held up as something/someone to which members of a monolithic notion of Black community can aspire—especially Black children.[7]

Third, I deploy class to parse Black taste cultures as Black fans engage such language around their fandom of/for Copeland. As with Bourdieusian conceptualizations of taste, Black fans imagine Copeland's position within American Ballet Theatre as an "inevitable difference" from other dance companies with whom she could likely dance.[8] This fan-based distinction likely has its roots in at least two places. First, because Copeland's Black fans are keenly aware of her biographical details, they understand the ways *she* distinguishes between ABT and other companies. And second, the US Congress recognized ABT as "America's national ballet company" in April 2006, a nomenclatural distinction that seemingly places ABT above all others.[9] Black fans construe a company of arguably equal prestige, like New York City Ballet, as representing New York City, whereas American Ballet Theatre represents the entire nation. For Copeland's Black fans, her representational importance is national, not local. They, in a Bourdieusian sense, refuse other tastes, like DTH, in favor of ABT (as Copeland does in her memoir). In other words, Copeland, and her attendant Black fandom, is bound within the politics of her being a principal ballerina at ABT versus any number of other national or international ballet companies. While this chapter explores the contours of Copeland's Black fandom through class, visibility and representation are not absent from the discussion.

Fourth, the use of class is tied to how Copeland's Black fans blur the undoubtedly porous and problematic lines between high and low culture. Black Misty Copeland fans, like Copeland herself, place value on mainstream/white spaces as the norm. Copeland could, presumably, be as talented as she is in DTH, but it is that she is in the largely white ABT that most makes her "worthy" of their fandom. But unlike assimilation, in which Black folks are asked to subsume themselves into the norms of the culture, Black Misty Copeland fans attempt to shift the space through an evaluation of Copeland in affective ways (rather than technical ones) and through language. For example, at an ABT performance in Washington, DC, where Copeland danced the lead role in *Whipped Cream*, as the lights dimmed and a hush fell over the crowd, a Black woman leaned over to her Black male companion and said, "Here come Misty." In this utterance, the woman signaled not only that Copeland was the main attraction for her and her companion that evening, but the vernacular use of "here come" instead of "here comes," reveals the ways Black fans flatten the idea that one must perform and speak in certain ways to access "high" cultural events like ballet. Taken together, this chapter's multivalent use of class illuminates how fandoms intersect with Black joy, the politics of Black visibility, and distinction—or in a word: class.

This chapter principally asks why this group of Black people, who are mostly unfamiliar with ballet, chose to consider themselves fans of a Black ballerina. The question I ask is underpinned by the assertion that Copeland is no "regular" ballerina. She is a *Black* ballerina who is in an even rarer stratosphere: Black celebrity. Through my interviews with 12 self-professed Black Misty Copeland fans, I uncover the messy matrix of Black fandom, Misty Copeland, celebrity, Black visibility, and class. These interviews were conducted between May and November 2018 via phone. The 12 Black Misty Copeland fans I interviewed for this chapter ranged in age from 26 to 57 and lived in mostly major metropolitan areas including Detroit, Los Angeles, Washington, DC, Chicago, Atlanta, and Kansas City. Beyond racial identity, I used no selection criteria other than that each person needed to identify themselves as a Black Misty Copeland fan. My interviewees are all middle-class individuals based on income (between $50,000 and more than $100,000 per annum) and the attainment of a college degree, with many of them having completed advanced degrees. (See chapter sidebar for full details on each participant.)

Finding Black Misty Copeland fans was more challenging than finding the other Black fans I study in *Fandom for Us, by Us*. Some of the people I interviewed are Facebook friends, with varying degrees of closeness to me. Others were friends of friends who heard about the project. Still others were people I found at Copeland's performances. This chapter, unlike the others in this book, includes participant observation at live performances at which Copeland danced in Vail, Colorado; New

York City; and Washington, DC, as well as often brief conversations with Black patrons at these performances. It also engages social media posts from Black users (identified as such by their avatar or photo). In sum, my 12 Black fan interviews, alongside participant observation and an examination of the discourse surrounding her, help to paint a picture of how Misty Copeland's Black fandom is a mostly classed endeavor.

Getting Misty-Eyed: Misty Copeland and the Production of Celebrity

Copeland is certainly a ballerina, but she is also a star. And most prominent ballet dancers are what I call *specialized celebrities* rather than *cultural celebrities*. A specialized celebrity, as I am theorizing it here, is one who is well-known among those deeply connected to a particular industry. These celebrities are certainly talented, but are known to a particular, and often relatively small, fan base. For example, Isaac Stern, a famous violinist, is a specialized celebrity whose fame is (mostly) cloistered to those who are connected to classical music. Additionally, balletomanes (a term describing ballet fans) would certainly be able to rattle off the names of company dancers whom they cherish for their balletic abilities. A specialized celebrity's appeal is akin to Chris Rojek's theorization of *achieved celebrity*, a form of celebrity in which the star has attained their fame through "accomplishments" in "open competition."[10] Copeland is different. Certainly, she embodies the ideals of achieved celebrity and is talented. But Copeland is partly what Rojek calls an *attributed celebrity*, one whose fame is also the "result of the concentrated representation of an individual as noteworthy or exceptional by cultural intermediaries." For example, the *Los Angeles Times*' Laura Bleiberg reported that "Copeland is the biggest draw in dance right now, a crossover star with international reach."[11] Thus, she is what I am calling a cultural celebrity—a star whose fame extends beyond a particular cloister. For example, ballet dancer Mikhail Baryshnikov, like Copeland, became a cultural star through his defection from Russia but also via his work in films like *White Nights* (1985, dir. Taylor Hackford) and *Company Business* (1991, dir. Nicholas Meyer) as well as television series like *Sex and the City* (HBO, 1998–2004). Where cultural stardom, as I am deploying it here, differs from ascribed celebrity is in its attention to race generally, and Blackness specifically. Copeland, through cultural intermediaries, specifically engaged her celebrification, centering her Blackness in an overwhelmingly white artform for a Black fanbase. The distinctions I am making here are like those the stars of *Real Husbands of Hollywood* (BET, 2013–2016) made between "famous" and "Black famous." In an online video, series star Boris Kodjoe explained the terms:

> Black famous constitutes a celebrity of African American heritage that enjoys a certain degree of notoriety exclusively in the African American demographic whereas another celebrity of African American heritage will enjoy a certain degree of celebrity in a more general market demographic [thus making that celebrity just famous]. When they walk into a drug store in Kansas City, they will evoke the same reaction as if they walked into a drugstore in downtown Atlanta.[12]

To extend the metaphor, "Black famous" corresponds to a specialized celebrity like New York City Ballet's (City Ballet) Sara Mearns or ABT's Stella Abrera—talented ballerinas in their own right—who have a fandom mostly situated within the ballet world. Mearns currently has 84,200 followers on Instagram while Abrera has 57,200 followers. Conversely, Copeland is "famous" as judged not only by her 1.8 million Instagram followers, but also her status as a star of the documentary *A Ballerina's Tale* (2015, dir. Nelson George); author of *Firebird* (2014), the *New York Times* bestseller *Life in Motion: An Unlikely Ballerina* (2014), and *A Ballerina's Body* (2017), and her endorsement deal (from 2014 until 2021) with athletic apparel brand Under Armour. At the same time, large ballet companies like ABT and City Ballet encourage a star system through not only a ranking scheme (which most ballet companies use to differentiate the corps de ballet, soloists, and principal dancers), but advanced announcements about who will dance which roles. These announcements are typically made prior to the start of season ticket sales because the companies know that some patrons want to see particular dancers in particular roles. And Copeland is clearly a draw for some ABT patrons in ways other ballerinas are not. For example, model Chrissy Teigen posted on her since-deleted Instagram page that she took her daughter "to see Misty Copeland in *Nutcracker*." This syntactical configuration is different than going to see *Nutcracker* and

Misty Copeland happens to be dancing the lead role of Sugar Plum Fairy. It also demonstrates not only the ways Black fans see Copeland as a star but how they make classed distinctions about *who* they see dancing classical ballet.

When I saw Copeland dance the Pas de Deux from choreographer Christopher Wheeldon's contemporary ballet *After the Rain* at the 2017 Vail International Dance Festival's mixed bill, as soon as Copeland walked onto the stage, the audience erupted into applause. When she finished dancing, a standing ovation ensued. In the space between the Copeland standing ovation and the beginning of the next piece, chunks of people left the performance, indicating that perhaps Copeland dancing was the "thing" some folks came to see and that many of those who left were *Copeland* fans, not *ballet* fans.

Rock star Prince helped Copeland in the production of her cultural celebrity. As a *Pitchfork* writer argues, Prince "was an advocate and a puppet master, operating from a position of compassion and control: he sincerely wanted to give other artists a boost."[13] While "moonlighting" from ABT as a dancer for Prince (ABT only employs her—and its other dancers—for a reported 36-week contract), Copeland gained notice in his 2009 music video "Crimson and Clover"—the music video in which Black Misty Copeland fan Reggie, 48, first discovered her. Prince also invited her to take part in the summer dates of his 2010 "20Ten" European tour (while she was laid off from ABT), which was followed by select dates on his 2011 "Welcome 2" tour. Through Prince, Copeland was not *only* being exposed to Black Prince fans, but I argue for Copeland, this exposure was important for her crossover into even having a Black fan base. It is not that Copeland "moonlighted"—most dancers use their time off to pursue other projects, often as guest dancers with other ballet companies. But Copeland used her time off to embark on a tour with one of the great music icons, and in the process, orchestrated her ascent from specialized celebrity to cultural celebrity—known not only outside the world of ballet, but among Black people who ultimately took her up as a fan object.

At the same time, Copeland, then a soloist with ABT, used that popular success—or even notoriety among Black people—to begin driving the discourse about her "low" position within the company. Soloists in ballet companies are not the lead in a ballet but dance featured roles.

For example, rather than performing Mina, the love interest in the ballet *Dracula*, a soloist would be cast as Lucy, Mina's best friend. Or in cinematic terms, as a soloist, Copeland would potentially be nominated for an award as Best Supporting Actress, not as Best Lead Actress. Many of those who saw Copeland dance for Prince and in any of the other venues in which she danced outside of ABT, including *The Arsenio Hall Show* (syndicated, 1989–1994; 2013–2014), wondered why she was "only" a soloist because they thought her talent extraordinary. This was particularly acute for Black folks unfamiliar with the ins and outs of ballet companies and ballet technique. Copeland's Black fandom demonstrates how she became a cultural celebrity and along the way upended a celebrity relay in which she began as a specialized star among the mostly white field of balletomanes and expanded her fan base to include Black folks who were interested in the politics of her visibility within the (mostly) white ballet world.

To that end, many of Copeland's Black fans discovered her not through her "day job" at ABT, but through Copeland paratexts. Media studies scholar Jonathan Gray suggests that it is almost impossible for the main text—in this case, Copeland—to "serve as the only source of information about the text. And rather than simply serve as extensions of a text, many [. . .] items are filters through which we must pass on our way to [. . .] our first and formative encounters with the text."[14] Courtenay, 52, first learned of Copeland when she saw a magazine cover. She says, "It wasn't even that I read the article, but I saw her pose in the magazine, and it drew my attention." Similarly, Jordan, 26, although she is a dancer herself, discovered Copeland not through ballet but via *Today* (NBC, 1952–present). Jordan says, "On *Today* they were discussing [Copeland] as a ballerina who was breaking barriers, and that was important to me." Reggie also discovered Copeland through means other than ABT. He says, "Actually, I saw her back in '09, I believe . . . with Prince. I saw the photos of them performing together, and when I saw her, she was so into the performance. Some of the different moves she was completing were just so intriguing. I was like, 'I have to know who she is.' That started [my fandom]." Courtenay, Jordan, and Reggie illuminate how Copeland has become a cultural celebrity whose celebrity extends beyond the relatively elitist (and white) walls of the ballet world. And importantly, while her fandom originates in other spaces, for these

Black fans, their—what might be called—paratextual fandom transitions them to ABT to see Copeland perform. Or, as Reggie says, seeing her in other venues first functioned as a "gateway drug" to his engagement with Copeland's live ballet performances with ABT. And it is important that for Reggie, and Black fans by extension, Copeland is a gateway drug to a deeper dive into ABT and Copeland, not necessarily a deeper dive into Black ballet dancers across the dance landscape. In this way, class shapes how Black fans engage with Copeland and ballet writ large.

Here Come Misty: Visibility, Blackness, and Ballet

Copeland's 2015 promotion to principal dancer, her Blackness, and her very existence within the ranks of ABT have been cause for consternation among some "real" (read: white) balletomanes. Copeland's star text—through her autobiography, interviews, and public appearances—positions her as a dancer who started ballet lessons late (at age 13) and whose body type is not historically associated with ballet. However, while Black fans, who came to ballet because of Copeland's presence within the artform, praise her talent and ability, some white balletomanes believe Copeland is unfit to dance in ABT, chiefly because of her inability to perform 32 consecutive turns (called fouettés), which are often required of the lead ballerina in many classical ballets like *Swan Lake*, *Don Quixote*, and *La Bayadere*. Twitter (now X) user @Miss_Hokie suggested that Copeland's inability to successfully complete these turns (classical ballets in ABT's repertoire are typically rechoreographed for Copeland to omit these turns) demonstrates that she is "the WORST and why it's an embarrassment to @ABTBallet to even have her on the roster, much less a principal dancer." While this (white-presenting based on avatar) user may be engaging in some semblance of hyperbole, it partly lays bare the collision of the racial politics of Copeland's body in a blindingly white artform and her Black fandom. Her Black body is partly configured as ill-fitting within ballet, or what American studies scholar Nicole Fleetwood theorizes as excess flesh because its presence is "constructed as having/being 'too much' in relation to the ideals of white femininity" within ballet.[15] In short, Black fans take up Copeland's "ill-fitting" Black body as a sign of #BlackExcellence because its "too

Figure 1.2. Me in ballet class at Joffrey Ballet (1994). © Donald Ewers. Photo used with permission of the estate of Donald Ewers.

muchness" is a neoliberal symbol of progress not just for Copeland, but for Blackness broadly construed.

My personal experience in the 1990s attests to the general lack of color within ballet. I finished high school at Interlochen Arts Academy, an arts boarding school in northern Michigan, and my first year there, I was one of only two Black dance students, and the only Black dance student in my final year. My time training at Joffrey Ballet found me, again, as the only Black ballet dancer (although there were some Hispanic and

Latin-descended dancers), and I was one of two Black (both male) ballet dancers at the University of Utah. And while I often deride the mantra "representation matters," for some folks, it does.

Kimberly, 55, suggests that while she grew "up in a family where I've been exposed to the arts and the culture," she "was always thinking in the back of my mind, [. . . that] I don't see us out there." And for her, visibility, particularly in the arts, matters. In many ways, Black fans, like Black audiences generally, believe that Black images amplified through mediated discourse can effectively show Black people, and especially Black children, the possibilities of Blackness itself. In other words, for Kimberly, not seeing "us out there" in "high" cultural forms is configured as troubling, if not altogether problematic. Similarly, Instagram user CreatedByKisha posted a photo of her daughter emulating a photo from Copeland's Edgar Degas–inspired 2016 photo shoot for *Harper's Bazaar*. CreatedByKisha says that her daughter loves ballet, but "in the few classes she has taken, there has been no one in her class that looks like her. This is why I think she is so intrigued with Misty Copeland."[16] Thus, for CreatedByKisha, visibility matters to her daughter, and through Copeland, she sees something that seemed an impossibility become possible. For these Black women, visibility is not a trap, as cultural theorist Michel Foucault asserts.[17] Rather, the "right" kind of visibility, for example, Misty Copeland, is configured as a gateway to imagining and harnessing the possibilities of Black excellence.

Misty Copeland's visibility within ABT has demonstrably changed not just who is on the stage at the ballet, but who is in the ballet audience. Copeland's cultural celebrity has resulted in some Black people becoming interested in ballet, like CreatedByKisha's daughter. Similarly, Jordan, 26, was familiar with ABT but says that she "started to really notice the company and pay attention to what performances they would be performing throughout the year once I found out that Misty Copeland was one of their principal dancers." In other words, Jordan's interest in ABT is driven by a visibility politic in which her interest in Copeland drives a broader interest in ABT because Copeland is a principal dancer on their roster. This interest is, obviously, bound within capitalism, in which the consumption of Copeland's performances is tied to the output of capital, but it is also deeply rooted in the pleasures Black fans, like Jordan, derive from seeing Copeland on the stage as a

Figure 1.3. Instagram post of Black girl emulating Misty Copeland's Degas-inspired photos. Photo and post used with permission of poster.

principal dancer ranked above a host of other white ballerinas within the company. At the same time, many of Misty Copeland's Black fans, like my parents when they came to see me dance, are not well-versed in the intricacies of ballet. While I want to be careful not to reinscribe high/low cultural distinctions that suggest enjoying and consuming particular artforms requires one to be learned, I want to suggest that Copeland's Black fans often operate from a space of affective attachment rather than knowledge of the artform in which she has excelled. For example, on a Facebook thread, a friend posted a photo of Copeland in a grand plié à la second en pointe from a 2017 *Paper* magazine photo shoot. One of his friends posted "Now that's talent." On the one hand, it certainly takes some modicum of talent to be able to wear pointe shoes and effectively execute ballet while wearing them. On the other hand, that Copeland, a principal dancer with ABT, is en pointe is perhaps overstating the price of admission to the category "talented." Thus, part of what I want to point to in this chapter are the ways Copeland's Black fandom is often tied into a politics of visibility and affect, not necessarily knowledge of the artform in which she excels. And that affective attachment to Copeland segues into the ways Black fans use

Figure 1.4. Gift shop display at the National Museum of African American History and Culture featuring Misty Copeland's Barbie doll and book. Photo taken by author.

class to justify their Copeland fandom and distinguish between Copeland and any number of other Black dancers.

When I saw Copeland dance in both New York (as the eponymous lead in Sir Kenneth MacMillan's *Manon*) and in Washington, DC (as the Praline Princess in *Whipped Cream*), I had never seen so many Black people at the ballet outside of a DTH performance. And particularly in DC, there were several Black children, mostly Black girls, who had been corralled to come to the ballet, not necessarily to see *Whipped Cream*, but to see Misty Copeland dance. According to one of the women who had organized the group, earlier that day, this group of visiting children had gone to the National Museum of African American History and Culture, where a Copeland merchandise display (with her doll and her book *Life in Motion*) was featured prominently in the gift shop with Gabrielle Douglas's doll and books.

MISTY'S BLACK FANS

Courtenay was born in 1971 and lives in Atlanta, although she is a Detroit native. She is a single mother of one adult child and makes between $40,000 and $59,999 per year. Discovering Copeland first on the cover of a consumer magazine, Courtenay did not "even [read] the article but seeing her pose in the magazine drew my attention." In this way, then, Courtenay was drawn to Copeland's presence and, discovered Copeland not through ballet, but through a consumer-facing publication, thus demonstrating how Copeland is a cultural, rather than a specialized, celebrity. Courtenay is my sister's friend from junior high school and wanted to talk to me about Copeland when she heard about the project from my sister.

Gary was born in 1965. He hails from Atlanta, but currently lives in Kansas City. Gary earns between $60,000 and $74,999 per year as a modern dance instructor and choreographer. Gary is drawn to Copeland because of "the physicality and the athleticism that she brought to [ballet] and how it had made the classics look different. Like made all of it look a little bit more, to my eye, athletic. I love what the Black body does. And so, no matter what the dance is, I love what the Black body does for it." As a modern dance instructor and choreographer, Gary feels drawn to the ways Copeland "Blackens" classical ballet movement in a way that is, intangible, but deeply affective. I first met Gary because he is a friend of my first modern dance teacher.

Jaketta was born and raised in Detroit. She is 47 and makes more than $100,000 per year. A married mother of two, Jaketta is a friend from junior high school, who, coincidentally, danced in the same dance group as I did at Detroit's Vetal Middle School. As a Misty Copeland fan, Jaketta appreciates "her being [at ABT], and I don't want to take away from her accomplishment because I think it's huge. But I struggle with intention. [...] Is she just the token Negro? Is that good too? [...] Yes, she's a Black woman, but where are the dark-skinned girls? Are there any dark-skinned girls who can do ballet? So I struggle with some of those things." Jaketta astutely picks up on the politics of Copeland's skin color, a topic to which I will return later in the chapter. For now, it is important to recognize that while Jaketta, a dark-skinned Black woman herself, is a Misty Copeland fan, her fandom is not uncritical of the larger ballet system that privileges lighter skin, particularly among Black women.

Johnique responded to a Twitter post in which I was looking for Black Misty Copeland fans. She was born in 1983 and lives in the Chicago suburbs where she annually makes between $60,000 and $74,999. As a Black fan, Johnique took a sort of fan pilgrimage to New York with a friend to see Copeland dance. She says, "We wanted to see her in her home space. [...] We did see that she was [performing] somewhere a little bit closer, but we just wanted to see her in her home." Johnique's pilgrimage to see Copeland at the Met in New York is different from those pilgrimages in which Rebecca Williams suggests "all fans at a specific important place can be seen as equal and as able to connect with one another," where "fans' ordinary markers of identity such as age, class or gender cease to be important and connection with other fans depends only on a shared sense of belonging and solidarity." Rather, there are differences: Johnique is there for Copeland because both are Black women within the politics of visibility. And while some balletomanes may be there to see Copeland, for most, the ballet, not Copeland, is what they have paid to see.

Jordan, a 26-year-old Detroit native, earns between $60,000 and $74,999 per year. She is a dancer and responded to my Twitter solicitation for Misty Copeland fans. Jordan considers herself a Misty Copeland fan because, she says, "I love her. I love what she represents and like I said, just for her to be a young Black woman who happens to be really, really talented and skilled in her style of dance. I love that about her, and I just admire her for that. And I hope to continue my dance path and be as much like her as possible." Jordan, like many of Copeland's Black fans, see her as a role model.

I have known **Kali** since the early 1990s when she and I danced at O'Day School of Dance in Detroit. Kali currently lives in Washington, DC, and earns more than $100,000 per year. Kali is 44 and discovered Copeland via social media. "I can't remember if it was Facebook or Twitter, but it was social media. Somebody posted something and they were like, 'Oh, it reminds me of you,'" because of her past as a dancer.

I met **Keisha** at a Washington, DC, ABT performance where Copeland danced Praline Princess in *Whipped Cream*—which was the first time she had seen Copeland dance live. She says, "It was just phenomenal just to see [Copeland perform live], like I was saying, the amount of children, and you could see their instructors were taking the children out to the ballet and to see Black girls and the faces . . . their faces just lit up like Christmas lights. You could feel their energy." Keisha was born in 1984 and earns more than $100,000 per year.

Kimberly was born in 1968 and lives in Brea, California, 33 miles southeast of Los Angeles. I met Kimberly through the Misty Copeland Facebook fan page. Kimberly makes between $75,000 and $99,999 per year and first discovered Misty Copeland on April 13, 2011, when she performed alongside Prince on *Lopez Tonight* (TBS, 2009–2011). Kimberly remembers seeing Copeland and thinking that "her grace and her poise was amazing. And of course, we both know that us African Americans are not represented in the art of ballet. I was like, 'Oh, wow, that girl is going to go far.'" As I will detail throughout this chapter, Kimberly is similar to many Copeland fans who discovered her not through her work with American Ballet Theatre, but through broader public outlets like television programs, magazine covers, and ad campaigns.

I also met **Priscilla** through the Misty Copeland Facebook fan page. Priscilla is a 54-year-old former dancer who currently lives in Long Beach, California. She makes more than $100,000 per year and says that, as a former professional dancer, she is drawn to Copeland because. "I understand Misty's struggles, being Black and dancing for a ballet company and lead dancer was something not heard of [and] she broke that stigma. I loved the fact that she made it to the top as the first Black principal dancer." Like many of the Black fans I interviewed throughout this chapter, there is a slippage between the ways Copeland's historic achievement with ABT is construed as not being specific to the company but to ballet as an entire artform. In other words, Copeland is the first Black woman to be principal dancer at ABT, not the first Black woman to be a principal dancer at a major ballet company—that distinction belongs to Lauren Anderson at Houston Ballet.

I went to Renaissance High School in Detroit with **Reggie**, and while we were not necessarily close friends, we knew each other and ran in some adjacent circles. Reggie is 48 years old, lives in Detroit, and is currently working on his doctorate in divinity. He makes between $75,000 and $99,999 per year and describes Copeland as his "gateway drug" to ballet. He says, "I honestly don't have the background [in ballet] to rattle off certain iconic performers. She's really one of the first [I have paid attention to]. She makes me want to know more about [ballet]." Thus, as I explore throughout this chapter, many of Copeland's Black fans come to ballet *because* of her, and often learn about ballet as they dive deeper into their Copeland fandom.

Stephanie, a mother of two, lives in the Detroit metro area and is 48 years old. I met Stephanie my senior year of high school at Interlochen Arts Academy, where she was a photography major. Stephanie makes more than $100,000 per year. Stephanie paid particular attention to Copeland because she sees Copeland as part of an "age of wokeness with people being aware of [race]. And I feel like Black people have been having some good years in terms of recognizing Black excellence in different fields." Stephanie connects Copeland to a longer history of Black excellence, and, as such, considers herself a Black Misty Copeland fan.

Tameka lives in Washington, DC, and I met her at the Kennedy Center performance of *Whipped Cream*. A 50-year-old mother to one daughter, she makes more than $100,000 per year. She was initially introduced to Copeland by her nine-year-old daughter. She says, "my daughter [...] had to do a black history project. So, my thing was for her, 'I want you to pick someone that everyone doesn't know off the top of their head. I want you to pick someone that means something close to you that you can relate to, and someone that's still alive.' She picked Misty Copeland. And I helped her with her research for the project, I got intrigued myself!" Tameka, again, demonstrates the ways that the Black Copeland fans with whom I spoke did not discover Copeland at the ballet, but instead, discovered Copeland and then went to the ballet to see her.

Fandom, Class, and American Ballet Theatre

In the United States, there are more than 700 professional ballet companies. These companies range in size (and location) from the eight dancers in Ballet Des Moines to the 98 dancers in City Ballet. Like consumer brands, each ballet company carries a particular cachet not only among other dancers, but among those who patronize them. In other words, no ballet company has an intrinsic value greater than another; rather it is that those who choose to patronize these companies (or choose one company over others) imbue them with value and create a classification system that distinguishes one company from another. Ballet Des Moines is no "worse" than City Ballet; but for most balletomanes, and likely members of the general public, the assumption is that City Ballet dancers are "better" than those in Ballet Des Moines because City Ballet represents a major metropolis with 18.8 million residents whereas Des Moines has a population of 552,000. These assumptions manifest in the distinctions Black fans make about Copeland's position within ABT. As Stephanie, 48, details:

> It's like if Misty Copeland is a principal at New York City Ballet. I feel like there are bigger dance companies, there are smaller ones. I feel like for me [. . .] when you hear American Ballet Theatre you're like, "Oh, that's a pretty decent-sized company, and she's the principal, like, that's great." You know? I feel like, in terms where you can be great, it's important. Can you be the mayor of New York, or can you be the mayor of Detroit or Des Moines, Iowa, or Wichita, Kansas. It's just a matter of like how big is this thing that you're in charge of, or that you're at the forefront of. When I think about her being at ABT, I think like, that's kind of a big deal. Whereas, if you were like, well Misty Copeland is a principal at Wichita Ballet Theatre, I would be like, "Oh, well good for her, well great." Like . . . it would mean a lot less in terms of notoriety [. . .] I think when you talk about ABT versus Dance Theatre of Harlem or even Alvin Ailey, I think you're talking about her basically pushing her way into a white space where they have not traditionally [. . .] accepted [Black ballet dancers].

At least three threads are worth examining in detail here. First, Stephanie distinguishes between ABT and other, "lesser" companies. Like Bourdieu claims, the distinctions Stephanie makes "are the practical affirmation of an inevitable difference" between DTH, Alvin Ailey American Dance Theater (Ailey), and the fictional Wichita Ballet Theatre.[18] Put another way, when distinctions between these ballet companies "have to be justified, they are asserted [. . .] by the refusal of other tastes."[19] ABT is different from and better than DTH, Ailey, and Wichita Ballet Theatre because Stephanie places these ballet companies in contradistinction to one another based partly on geography—Wichita is not New York City—and partly on the racial makeup of the companies.

Secondly, Stephanie distinguishes between Copeland's position in ABT from primarily Black dance companies like DTH and Ailey in racialized terms. For Stephanie, Copeland's exceptionalism is rooted in her being in a space that has historically not welcomed Black dancers. Similarly, Keisha, 39, says, "I think she sets herself apart from the Dance Theatre of Harlem, you know, Alvin Ailey dancers, only because of the fact that she's kind of in the . . . if she were to be in the Dance Theatre of Harlem, she would be just another number." Keisha finds Copeland exceptional because she is not in a company that has several Black dancers. The classed distinction of Copeland's Black body "invading" a primarily white space gestures toward not only her #BlackExcellence, but the ways Black visibility is one of the cornerstones of Copeland's Black fandom. At the time of our interview there were only two Black dancers in ABT: Copeland and Calvin Royal III, who joined the company in 2010, and was promoted to principal in 2020, making him the third Black principal dancer with ABT—the first was Ailey alum Desmond Richardson, who joined for one season in 1997 primarily to dance ABT's ballet *Othello* and not have to resort to using Blackface for the ballet's titular character.[20] At the same time, Copeland's Black fans perform the work sociologists Fleming and Roses suggest Black cultural capitalists do: they grant higher status to Black artists working in primarily white cultural spaces because of historical Black exclusion from such spaces.[21] Thus, Copeland's Black fans approach Copeland as valuable aesthetically because she is a principal dancer with ABT *and* is nearly the lone Black body in a sea of mostly white bodies.[22]

Third, Stephanie identifies Copeland as *the* principal dancer at ABT. The use of the article "the" suggests her singularity. Certainly, at the time of my interview with Stephanie, Copeland was *the* Black principal dancer at ABT, but she was one of 16 principal dancers with the company. Similarly, Johnique suggests that part of Copeland's achievement is that "there's not a lot of Black women in ballet, and yet [Misty] being the head [of ABT]" is an achievement. Drawing attention to the use of "the" and "head" highlights that many of Copeland's Black fans are coming to ballet for Copeland, and as such, their knowledge of how ballet companies function is limited. In this way, then, their Black fandom is partly predicated on a double exceptionalism: Copeland is not only the first Black women promoted to principal at the company, but their belief is also that she is also the "head" of the company.

Keisha previously had dance familiarity with only Ailey, a primarily Black modern dance company. On the one hand, Ailey is, without question, a premiere American dance institution. On the other hand, modern dance has often been a space where Blackness has flourished. Aside from Alvin Ailey, Black women like Katherine Dunham and Pearl Primus innovated modern dance in ways similar to white modern dance pioneers including Martha Graham and Isadora Duncan. Particularly within ballet worlds, modern dance is often (falsely) construed as failure: those who cannot succeed in ballet turn to modern dance as a consolation prize. Thus, Copeland's Black fans use class to distinguish her from modern dancers and modern dance companies. Johnique, 40, says:

> I think what Misty did by doing ballet is she stepped into an arena that predominantly is not ethnically diverse [. . .] No, you don't see that. We love Alvin Ailey [. . .]. They come to a university that's probably maybe 10 minutes away from my house and we go see [Ailey] there. And they are absolutely phenomenal; culturally [they] speak to who we are as African American men and women. Just the artistry there, is phenomenal [. . .]. And there's a certain level of elegance that goes with it. But everyone expects that. "Oh, Alvin Ailey's going to be mainly Black people, Caribbean people, African people. There's going to be brown people at Alvin Ailey." We expect that . . . I think with Misty [. . .] you have this brown woman as the head of American Ballet Theatre at the Met doing ballet like, "Okay. Okay, now what is this about? We're doing something different here." And what I think she did was she said to mainstream America that African American women are not going to be stereotyped in one particular form of dance. We're not going to do that because guess what? We are bigger than you putting us in this little box over to the side and saying we only can dance this way because that's truly not who we are.

Johnique suggests that Copeland is distinguished via her position within a ballet company that has historically been filled with white dancers. Thus, unlike modern dance companies like Alvin Ailey, where

Copeland's Blackness would have been more expected, it is Copeland's Black body in a white space that Johnique contends deserves celebration and fandom. It also adds to Copeland's distinction. Bourdieu asserts that dialectically the distinction enjoyed by certain objects is achieved via the devaluation of others, thus employing a system of binary oppositions.[23] Copeland is partly exceptional because she is not in Ailey doing modern dance—she defies stereotype and expectations for Black women by being "the head" of ABT. Similarly, Tameka, 50, posits, "I think that if she was [in] a ballet group that was all African American, she probably would not be standing out as much as she stands out now." For both Johnique and Tameka, it is not that Black dance companies like Ailey or DTH are "bad"; it is that Blackness within Ailey and DTH are quotidian. Thus, part of Copeland's Black fandom is predicated on Copeland bringing Black fans to ballet rather than Black folks already being balletomanes and becoming Copeland fans in the process. In short, the intersection of Copeland's Black fandom and class lies at her being a Black ballerina rather than a Black modern dancer *and* working within a mostly white ballet company rather than a mostly Black one. Stephanie, 48, adds:

> While Misty Copeland clearly is not the President [Barack Obama], it at least opens one more thing that we are not excluded from in terms of notoriety. Because, I mean, she may very well be the first, I mean principal in terms of being Black, but she certainly is not the only Black ballerina out there. That's just not true, but I also think that what the media pays attention to is important. The fact that they've kind of latched onto her is important, because [. . .] it does put Black people in ballet where people may not have thought that. Or, I would think that Black people often associate Black dancers with more modern dance, more Alvin Ailey or Dance Theatre of Harlem.

An artist herself, Stephanie understands that the interpretation of Copeland's star text as the *only* Black principal ballerina in the history of dance is false and partly bound within mediated discourse around Copeland (a discourse Copeland actively encouraged until around the 2021 release of her book *Black Ballerinas: My Journey to*

Our Legacy). Black ballerinas including (but certainly not limited to) Lauren Anderson (Houston Ballet), Debra Austin (New York City Ballet and Pennsylvania Ballet), Janet Collins (Ballet Russe de Monte Carlo), Virginia Johnson (Dance Theatre of Harlem), and Raven Wilkinson (Ballet Russe de Monte Carlo) had been principal ballerinas within ballet companies before Copeland. However, Stephanie extricates Copeland from spaces where her body might be more expected to appear, like Alvin Ailey or DTH. It is the defiance of expectations that activates class as a Black fandom practice around Copeland for Stephanie and Johnique. Copeland is not *supposed* to be in ABT. Although both DTH and Alvin Ailey are extraordinarily difficult companies for Black dancers to gain admittance, there is the assumption that admittance is easier because both companies welcome Black dancers within their ranks.

Gary, 58, understands the importance of Copeland's position within ABT, but simultaneously wishes "that she was part of an organization like Dance Theater of Harlem and could bring her celebrity to an organization like that." Gary partly recognizes the classed distinction between DTH and ABT, particularly in its funding. ABT was founded in 1939, has been performing constantly since then, and currently employs 79 dancers. DTH, founded in 1969, was on a hiatus from 2004 until 2012 because of financial troubles, and it currently employs 16 dancers. Gary implicitly understands that Copeland's dancing with DTH would bring funding that could secure the future of America's only ballet company that has historically employed ballet dancers of color. He understands how Copeland's status and celebrity would benefit DTH even as it is unlikely that many of her fans would be her fans if she were a ballerina with DTH rather than ABT.

This section has demonstrated how class, as a Black fandom practice, manifests in the ways Copeland's position as a principal ballerina within American Ballet Theatre drives fan engagement. Black fans place importance on Copeland as a dancer with ABT over any other number of ballet companies or modern dance companies. On the one hand, Copeland's Black fandom can seem like work. Black fans use their labor to amplify Copeland's celebrity in a mostly white ballet company and subsume Copeland into a broader discourse about #BlackExcellence. On the other hand, Black fans also find joy in seeing Copeland's Black body excel. While they may not know the technical jargon that balletomanes do, they appreciate and luxuriate in the beauty of Copeland's dancing Black body. In the next section, through my interviews with Copeland's Black fans, I build on this chapter's theorization of class by engaging in the ways they understand Copeland as a "classy" role model.

In a Class by Herself: Misty Copeland as Role Model

Copeland's position in ABT versus a discursively "lesser" ballet company also distinguishes her as a role model for her Black fans. As I have argued elsewhere, Black fan objects as role models intertwines love for the fan object and hunger for visibility. "For [many] Black fans, images cease to necessarily 'just' be reduced to their 'positive' or 'negative' attributes; rather, fan objects are chosen based upon their fitness as a role model."[24] Relinking to Copeland's status as a cultural celebrity, she often reposts Instagram posts, like CreatedbyKeisha's, in which Black children are emulating her. Copeland reposted two such images—one from a Stuart Weitzman campaign in which Copeland posed, and a second in which she is with Calvin Royal III as they prepared for their debut in *Romeo and Juliet* (a debut that was canceled because of the COVID-19 pandemic). In each of these sets of photos, the children's parents demonstrate that Copeland (and in one instance, perhaps Calvin Royal III, although @AndreasFireCurls, the original poster, did not hashtag him as she did with Copeland) are suitable role models for their Black children.

How this process differs from the ways Black folks engage with role models for a film like *Black Panther*, which I discuss in chapter 2, is in its tethering to the real and its decoupling from consumption practices. Black folks can see Copeland in the real world via her countless public appearances, interviews on television programs and in magazines and newspapers, and as a guest judge on dance competition series like *So You Think You Can Dance* (Fox, 2005–2022). Put simply, Black fans *can* pay for Copeland's performances, books, and her Barbie doll, but their fandom is not predicated on that as it is with *Black Panther*. In addition, Copeland is not a fictional character. She is a living, breathing person. Unlike *Black Panther*, it is Copeland (presumably) who posts on her social media accounts, and while *Black Panther* had a particular shelf life in which Disney and Marvel were interested in maintaining the social media accounts linked to the film, Copeland can post as long as her fans are hungry for content.

Copeland's ABT "platform," for Black fans like Kali, 44, allows Copeland to "put the spotlight on herself and be like, 'Look at me. I have come out and I've had all kinds of adversities. Here I am and it's going to be known.' I think when people see that, they get inspired by it. Not necessarily that you want to be the next president or the next prima ballerina, but like, 'Okay, look what [Black people] can do.'" Similarly, Gary, 58, says, "To me, she was like, 'Oh, so we're going to [center race in ballet], I'm going to write this book and I'm going to represent myself this way and I'm going to make some commercials and I'm going to inspire some Black kids and I'm going to do all of this stuff, and that is going to put me at an advantage.'" Kali and Gary both understand how Copeland's celebrity is produced through cultural intermediaries, but they also maintain the importance of her celebrity and the ways it inspires Black people broadly, and Black children specifically. Like Copeland's 2014 Under Armour campaign, in which she declared, "I will what I want," Copeland presumably allows Black fans, and other Black people by extension, to understand that hard work and persistence are the keys to Black success and structures their cultivated consumption of her. But more than that, Copeland's Under Armour campaign relies on a specifically American approach to bootstrapping. In this configuration, Copeland was promoted to principal ballerina because of her hard work, and racial—or any other kinds of barriers—no longer exist in an allegedly post-racial world.

Copeland's promotion and position at ABT puts her in a class by herself among her Black fans. Within Black fan discourse, Copeland broke a barrier that had previously been understood as precluding Black (female) dancers from the upper echelons of American ballet companies. It is partly that notion of breaking barriers that leads to the classed nature of Black fans' understanding of Copeland as different from other ballerinas and even other Black ballet dancers who currently occupy the ranks—and broke similar barriers—at companies like Boston Ballet and Ballet West. Jordan, 26, says:

> Misty Copeland [. . .] basically just defied the odds and is just a really good example for a young Black woman, like myself, who are pursuing

Figure 1.5. Two Instagram posts featuring Black children emulating Copeland (and, in one, Calvin Royal III, the other Black principal dancer at American Ballet Theatre).

calvinroyaliii

Liked by **mistyonpointe** and **703 others**

calvinroyaliii This picture says it all 🤍 #Repost @mistyonpointe
. . .
How adorable is this!!!!! 🤍🤍🤍🤍🤍
@andreasfirecurls To my dance partner for life, my brother.
What do you think of our recreation?
@mistyonpointe #dancepose #mybrother

Figure 1.5. (*Continued*)

dance [. . .]. Like taking classes when I was growing up, I didn't really see a lot of Black dancers in my dance classes. [. . .] So, seeing that story about her and how she basically kind of went through the same thing I did, you know, just [the] experience being at ABT and not really being represented as well as she probably would have liked to be. And just her just getting a chance to become a principal ballerina. [. . .] And it inspired me to continue to press through and take dance classes even though I might not be represented in those styles of dance, but just really like go for it.

Jordan specifically connects the notion of "breaking barriers" with Copeland's fitness as a role model for young Black women—regardless of whether they are aspiring dancers or not. For Jordan, Copeland is useful for Black women who are not represented in particular fields—whether dance, business, or sport—to "go for it" despite being underrepresented. And it is Copeland's hard work and determination that Black women should take from Copeland's story and apply to their own professional paths.

At least two things distinguish Copeland from other Black ballet dancers. First, those ballet companies, in Black fans' imaginations, and as discussed earlier, represent cities and regions—not the entire country. Second, unlike other Black dancers, as Kali, 44, says, Copeland "marketed herself[. . . .] That is so commendable that she's just like, 'I'm about to make this happen.' So, just her constant PR work, like the constant posts on Facebook [. . .] the advertisements that she's done." Kali continues by suggesting that, ultimately, like Copeland's Under Armour campaign, Copeland "will[ed] what she want[ed]." Concomitantly, Copeland's self-commodification is part of how she distinguishes herself among ballet dancers generally and Black ballet dancers specifically. It is partly why Black fans misunderstand Copeland's historicity—Copeland is the first Black female principal ballerina at ABT, but not the first Black female principal ballerina writ large.

But Copeland's visibility—at ABT—is part of what makes her a role model for Black fans. For example, Priscilla, 54, calls Copeland "a role model for young Black girls to go after their dreams. Whatever it might be . . . She's a perfect role model; beautiful, Black with determination. We can conquer whatever life throws in our direction." Reggie, 48, adds, "I think for young African American women I would see her as a tremendous role model." In both Priscilla's and Reggie's configurations of Copeland as role model, Copeland's reach, like her star persona, extends beyond the cloistered ballet world. For Priscilla, Copeland stands in for not only Black excellence, but the idea that anything is possible if one wills what they want.

Johnique, 40, uses Copeland as a role model for her children who are majorette dancers. She has them watch online clips of Copeland dancing to understand "how you should stand when you're resting, in terms of being in tune with your posture, ensuring that you're aligned, looking at lines when you're doing your stance [. . .] I have used her. Like, 'Y'all look at her. She's the greatest ballerina. If y'all could mimic her, we'll be good.'" At least two things are worth expanding upon in Johnique's comments about Copeland as a role model. First, Johnique uses Copeland as a model for good dance—not just ballet, but understanding, and trying to get her children to understand, the importance of body alignment and posture. Thus, Copeland, because of the way her fame has functioned outside ballet, stands in for all dance/dance forms in terms of role modeling. Second, and related, Johnique suggests that Copeland is the "greatest ballerina." While notions of "greatest" are subjective, it is worth noting that, for Johnique and many of the other Black Misty Copeland fans I interviewed, their knowledge of other ballerinas is limited. Here I want to highlight how Misty Copeland's Black fans are brought to ballet because of her, and they, thus, map the confluence of Black visibility, Copeland's rank within ABT, and their affective responses to her onto the notion of "greatest." In this configuration of class as a Black fandom practice, it is the convergence of two interwoven discourses: first, Copeland is configured as "the greatest" Black ballerina which justifies Black fans' engagement with her; second, Black fans elevate Copeland as more than simply a great ballerina, but one who is deemed worthy as a role model.

Stephanie, 48, says, as the mother of two Black girls she is "always happy to see Black representation in fields that we have not historically been in because I think it's important for little Black girls to feel like there's nothing they can't do. I like for them to see that everything is open to them, just like every little white girl and every little white boy feels like there's nothing they can't do, I would like for my girls to feel like there's nothing they can't do." For Stephanie, it is not necessarily that her daughters aspire to be ballerinas or even dancers. Rather, Copeland's utility as a role model is twofold. First, Copeland represents a crumbling system in which Blackness no longer disqualifies one from participation. Second, and related, Stephanie suggests that Copeland stands in for role model parity: white boys and girls have had exnominated, but white, Supermen and Wonder Women to whom they could model their life trajectories. For Stephanie, Copeland represents similar possibilities for Black children. Echoing this sentiment, former president Barack Obama, in a conversation with Copeland and *Time* magazine writer Maya Rhodan about race, gender, and success, remarked on Copeland's fitness as a role model, saying:

> as the father of two daughters, one of the things I'm always looking for are strong women who are out there [. . .] breaking barriers and doing great stuff. And Misty's a great example of that. Somebody who has entered a field that's very competitive, where the assumptions are that she may not belong. And through sheer force of will and determination and incredible talent and hard work she was able to arrive at the pinnacle of her field. And that's exciting.[25]

Obama's embrace of Copeland combines discourses about breaking barriers and bootstrapping to suggest—like her recent campaign with PassItOn.com in which her image is used alongside the ad copy "Picture yourself winning"—that success is about applying "sheer force of will" rather than overcoming systemic barriers.

Part of the classed distinctions related to Copeland's Black fans' selection of her as a role model is rooted in her Black body's being construed as atypical for ballet. Courtenay, 52, says Copeland represents "young girls who have a dream, and they may not look like that but they're trying to do it anyway." Courtenay situates Copeland as not only a role model but draws on Copeland's suggestion that she is a "curvy" ballerina and thus less fit for a career in ballet. When Courtenay says that those dreaming of a career in ballet "may not look like" stereotypic ballet dancers, she reinscribes the idea that ballet dancers simply must "will what [they] want." Copeland's fans do not "make up" that her body is not necessarily fit for dance. Rather, they mostly parrot the language she uses to describe herself. In her memoir, Copeland says that while she might be considered fat in the ballet studio—at five-foot-two and

Figure 1.6. Copeland in an ad for PassItOn.com in Chicago O'Hare Airport's Terminal 3. Photo taken by author.

typically weighing "just over a hundred pounds," she "wasn't fat on the streets of New York. I was desirable and attractive. In fact, my look—dark hair, brown skin, curvy physique—melded seamlessly into the urban rainbow."[26] Thus, as in American studies scholar Nicole Fleetwood's theorization, Copeland's "Black female body always presents a problem within" ballet, structured as it is "by racialized and gendered markings."[27] In this way, Copeland is understood as making her allegedly ill-fitting body work within "America's national ballet company."

In addition to her own affective bond with Copeland, Jaketta, 48, suggest that Copeland is important because her eight-year-old daughter "believes she's going to be the second principal ballerina for ABT . . . Now, she wants to be that because she saw Misty dance and she was like, 'Mommy, she's Black [. . .] I'm going to be the second principal ballerina for the . . . ,' she didn't say ABT, but she said for the ballet company. And I said, 'You know what? If you work hard, you point your toes, you'll be able to do it.' So specifically, [Copeland is] important because she allows Black people to dream." As media scholar C. Lee Harrington and her co-authors detail, media has historically exposed adolescents "to a wide variety of role models, allowing them to explore a range of possible selves in the transition from adolescence to adulthood."[28] Jaketta reveals the intertwining logics of Black fandom, class, and role modeling for her daughter. She sees Copeland's achievements as allowing her daughter to see possible career paths, thus positioning Copeland as a suitable role model for her daughter to choose. Tameka, 50, also sees Copeland as a role model for her daughter, saying, "As a mom, I don't want my daughter to look up to a person that is not something that I would want her to want to strive to be like down the line. So, with Misty Copeland, she's been that person for my daughter." En route to constructing Copeland as a role model, Jaketta and Tameka distinguish Copeland from other, less fit public figures whom their daughters might aspire to emulate. In their role as parent, both women understand that Copeland, as a principal dancer of a mainstream ballet company, is suitable for their daughters as a role model.

Taking Copeland as a role model does not end at adolescence. Jaketta, 48, sees Copeland as a role model for her adult self because of the ways Copeland's body "inspires" her to accept her own "curvy" and "muscular" body. She says that Copeland is "very muscular compared to most ballerinas. And I identify with her in that sense because as a muscular woman, I get that. Muscles aren't [supposed to be] feminine." Jaketta clearly understands that muscles are out of line with the ways women are "supposed" to look within broader culture. As Africana studies scholar Andrea Shaw argues, heteropatriarchal culture insists on "slenderness and delicacy" for white women.[29] Ballet is *still* an overwhelmingly white artform that centers white delicacy and slenderness generally, but especially through the canonization of waif-like roles in ballets like the titular character in *Giselle* (who dies because of a "weak heart") and Odette in *Swan Lake*. But as Obama suggests upon hearing Copeland describe herself as athletic, "I have to say as an outside[r . . .] When I hear that like your body type is considered sort of more athletic or large, you're tiny. For those of you who are watching, you may not be able to see. I mean, you're petite."[30] Thus, as media studies scholar Samantha Shepperd argues about the Black sporting body, "race and gender [. . .] become distilled through discourses and performances."[31] Because Black women are never imagined as ideally feminine—because they are not white—Copeland's just over 100-pound body is construed as muscular and therefore the antithesis of "proper" femininity. Because of that configuration, that Copeland achieved the highest rank within ABT with her imagined less-than-ideal physique ultimately positions her as a role model. Johnique, 40, says, "from a grown woman perspective, looking at Misty also becomes a reflection of the things that I also had to overcome." Kali, 44, sees Copeland as fearless and maps that onto her own life as a former dancer. "I made the safe decision to go to Michigan State [instead of pursuing a career in dance]. Now, looking at her story and seeing this as a role model, and I was just like, 'Wow.' Wondering what could have been my journey if I pursued [dance . . .] and not being afraid. I think that's one of the things that resonates with me: she went and she tried it even though there weren't necessarily any role models that were paving the way for her. [. . .] Looking back on my life, I was just like, 'I should have tried to see what would have happened. Could that have been me?' Who knows?"

For Jaketta, Johnique, and Kali, becoming a Copeland fan, and positioning her as a role model, illuminates how this process is, as Matt Hills details, "lived as self-narrative."[32] Jaketta sees her body type/shape depicted in Copeland. Johnique identifies her life narrative in Copeland's struggles. Kali sees a fearlessness in Copeland that makes her a role model. Copeland is partly in a class by herself because of her extraordinary balletic talent while also embodying the ethos that her exceptional qualities could exist in anyone who works hard enough. Copeland's Black fandom, then, manifests itself in the ways Black fans, in ways akin to bell hooks's theorization of Black women's negotiated reception practices, understand Copeland's frustrations as the only Black dancer at ABT (prior to Calvin Royal III's arrival in 2010) and, thus, claim Copeland as theirs.[33] But more than simply "claiming" Copeland, Black fans, particularly Black women fans, elevate her above other potential fan objects. Copeland's fandom is useful for these Black women to see themselves, and by extension Black women's and Black children's struggles: to be seen, to be heard, to be enough.

However, as media and cultural studies scholar Herman Gray warns, while representations of "Black achievement do recognize and effectively make visible Black presence and accomplishment in the national culture [. . .] they are no guarantors of progressive projects for racial justice [. . . . They] can just as easily be used to support political projects that deny any specific claim or warrant on the part of Black folk to experiencing disproportionately the effects of social injustice, economic inequality, racism, and so on."[34] Thus, while Copeland's achievements are great, and there are, indeed, more Black dancers in ABT than there have ever been, it remains to be seen if Copeland has truly opened the doors for the little Black girls for whom Black fans have larger dreams. But regardless of whether long-term change materializes within ABT and ballet more broadly, Misty Copeland's Black fans believe in the possibilities she represents and use classed distinctions to position her as an ideal role model for Blackness.

Class, Culture, and Copeland

Misty Copeland is what media scholar John Fiske calls a media figure—she is a "hyperreal person whose reality includes both a body . . . composed of flesh, bone, and blood, and a body of infinitely reproducible signifiers."[35] Copeland means different things to her Black fans—she is a role model, an athlete, a pioneer, and she wills what she wants. But, at base, Copeland and her Black fandom is a project organized around classed distinctions. Partly, the way class works with Copeland's Black fandom is through an elision of a Black ballet past. A long line of Black ballet dancers paved the way for Copeland.[36] They walked so Misty Copeland could run. They also danced in a much different time, before social and "spreadable" media.[37] Many danced in the immediate wake of a post–Civil Rights Movement era in which there was a cultural, political, and social move to downplay the importance of race. In fact, Debra Austin, who danced with City Ballet from 1971 to 1980, recounted to me that she was forbidden from talking to the press about being a Black ballerina, let alone one in a mostly white company. Fast-forwarding more than 40 years later, Copeland was not forbidden from talking to the press, and she hired a publicist to help highlight race and her initial failure to be promoted at ABT.

Within Black fandom, class works as a distinguishing feature that elevates Copeland among a growing list of her Black (particularly women) ballet contemporaries, including Katlyn Addison (Ballet West), Chyrstyn Fentroy (Boston Ballet), Nikisha Fogo (San Francisco Ballet), and Claudia Monja (Nashville Ballet), among others. It is not that these women can be evaluated as worse dancers than Copeland. Because they are principal ballerinas in their respective companies, they are obviously talented dancers. Rather, the classed distinctions that work among Copeland's fandom ranks them lower (and, quite frankly, illegible to many Black Misty Copeland fans) because they dance in regional- and city-based ballet companies whereas Copeland is a principal ballerina in "America's national ballet company." And, as I have argued throughout this chapter, the perceived *Americanness* of ABT creates a classed distinction for Copeland's Black fans.

Class as a Black fandom practice not only demonstrates how fans make a choice of one fandom object over another—that is relatively stable across fan practices. It demonstrates how broader cultural discourses structure Black fandom. That Copeland moved from her status as a specialized celebrity to a cultural one meant that she had reach beyond the "elite" halls of the Metropolitan Opera House in New York and into the concert arenas and onto television screens where Black folks could have seen her. And because Copeland was the first Black ballerina to use publicity to shift her celebrity status, in some ways, she (inadvertently, I believe) scorched the earth behind her such that upcoming Black ballerinas could not capture the Black public imagination in the ways she has. In other words, as the first Black ballerina to exploit publicity to her advantage, the second Black ballerina to do so has less news value.

As a classed fan object, Copeland, via her savviness, took ballet to "the (Black) people." In making herself and ballet visible and accessible to Black fans in ways they had not previously been, Copeland's Black fans do work similar to the work they do around Black athletes like Serena Williams (tennis), Tiger Woods (golf), and Gabrielle Douglas (gymnastics). These amazing athletes have certainly built on a longer legacy of Black folks in their respective sports. But the work these Black fans do around Copeland is rooted in her "firstness" (for them) and her ability to speak directly back to fans without the interference of cultural intermediaries via social media (although Copeland certainly uses these cultural intermediaries in her "official" publicity). Thus, Copeland has fashioned herself somewhat as "the people's ballerina" who centers race, and Black fans take her up as "the *Black* people's ballerina" because of what she means to/for Black visibility in white spaces. And in claiming Copeland as a Black woman who has achieved the highest possible rank within ABT, her Black fans also can shape their own Black identity through classed markers.

The next chapter builds on some of the aspects of *class* by discussing the second C of Black fandom: *clout*. While Copeland's Black fans mostly engage with her star text discursively, *clout* specifically engages the use of Black spending power to make Black fandom visible. As I discussed in the introduction, clout, for example, is not entirely divorced from class, as some of Copeland's Black fans indeed go to ABT performances in New York and when the company is on tour as a way to make their fandom legible. They show up to show ABT that they will spend their Black dollars to see Black ballerinas at the height of their balletic powers. And if ABT wants the Black dollar, elevating Black dancers within its ranks is the only way to capture that consumer segment. Put simply, Black fans will use class to distinguish Copeland from other Black ballet dancers in other companies, and once those distinctions are clear, they will use clout to ensure ABT does not close its doors to Black ballet dancers behind her.

2

Clout

Black Panther, *Doing It for the Culture,* and Black Fandom

Shortly after the release of *Black Panther* (2018, dir. Ryan Coogler), Jimmy Fallon, host of *The Tonight Show Starring Jimmy Fallon* (NBC, 2014–present), gathered Black folks to express the importance of *Black Panther* to one of the film's theatrical posters of its star, Chadwick Boseman. One man said, "But on a personal note, my father is African. He's from Ghana. He's a scientist. My mother, my sisters, brilliant African American women. So basically, everything that represents me was honored in this movie. I've seen the movie twice in theaters already and once on bootleg."[1] For this man, his direct lineage to Africa alongside the professional achievements of his family meant that *Black Panther* felt important to him, so important that he saw the film three times—spending his money to see it twice. In the same segment, another man said, "It means a lot to see a movie that's not like a Black movie but it's just a great American superhero movie with, you know, people who look like me." In this case, the notion that *Black Panther* did not necessarily center Blackness, but instead featured a "universal" story with Black characters that appealed to the masses, made the film important. While *Black Panther*'s characters might be understood as what Kristen Warner calls "plastic"—lacking heft and relying on Black audiences to labor to make the characters affectively feel Black—for this man, their "just happening to be" Black works to help him place *Black Panther* as an example of so-called "positive" representation.[2] Lastly, a woman declared that "as the mother of a young [Black] son, my son's childhood has been defined by Barack Obama, and now *Black Panther*, so thank you." In this configuration of the social good *Black Panther* does, the importance of Black male role models for Black children (especially male children) is paramount. And the importance of a film like *Black Panther* and its titular character are, for this woman, on par with other Black milestones like the election of the first Black president of the United States. While these folks could be fabricating their stories in exchange for 15 seconds of fame, their comments nonetheless set the stakes for what I want to explore in this chapter: the interlocking discourses around Black visibility, Black consumption practices, Black role models, and Black-cast films. In other words, this chapter is concerned with what I am calling *clout*. In its most basic definition, *clout* concerns the use of one's influence or power to effect change. I extend that definition of clout to help explain the relay between Black folks feeling seen in/by media industries *and* the compulsion to consume certain Black-cast films in theaters to demonstrate value as an audience/consumer segment. At the same time, the ultimate goal of Black fans' use of clout is invested in notions of Black futurity. As a Black fandom practice, clout's engagement with Black futurity is threefold: it is concerned with (1) the future of so-called "quality" Black-cast film production, (2) Afrofuturist textual themes, and (3) Black social production. In the first instance, clout is deployed to ensure not "just" the future of Black-cast films, but the future of *particular* Black-cast films that have high budgets and conform to a representational politic that can be considered (however problematic) as "positive" and "uplifting." While *Black Panther* is temporally separated by a century from the films called "uplift films," the ways clout is deployed as a reception response is similar. Film scholar Allyson Nadia Field argues that "uplift films" center narrative themes around "individual initiative, mutual assistance, social respectability, interracial cooperation, and economic independence" as a "strategy for promoting the advancement of African Americans."[3] Thus, clout, as an outgrowth of "uplift," signals not just the politics of capital (and expending said capital) but also the politics of representation. This usage of clout is also enmeshed in the logics of consumer citizenship, a topic to which I return shortly.

Second, clout, as a fannish practice, is partly enveloped in *Black Panther* as an Afrofuturist text. While all media texts are certainly polysemic and open, *Black Panther* includes Afrofuturist themes such that audiences and fans can easily sift through the narrative threads and images to decode the film Afrofuturistically. Communication scholars Beschara Karam and Mark Kirby-Hirst argue that "Afrofuturistic cinematic text[s] grant [B]lacks agency in the telling or retelling/reimagining their futures and revisiting or reimagining their past."[4] In imaging

Wakanda as an African nation untouched by colonialism, *Black Panther* attempts to retell a Black diasporic history that imagines Africa not as an uncivilized land that benefitted from colonialism (as media like the miniseries *Roots* [ABC, 1977] do), but as one that prospered in its absence. While all images within *Black Panther* (and media broadly) are empty signifiers, Afrofuturism as a textual property attempts to shape reception and fannish practices within the "dominant code" of the encoding/decoding process.[5] And, as I demonstrate throughout this chapter, Afrofutrism in its many valences shaped how Black fans used their clout toward ensuring the future of "quality" Black-cast media through *Black Panther* consumption.

Finally, Black social production and clout are tethered to Black futurity. Black consumption of *Black Panther* was tied to thinking about children and the available images they can consume. To be sure, a lot of the work done by Black *Black Panther* fans maps the hopes and dreams of visibility and resonance onto children—imagining Black children as unable to resist media's hypodermic needle of content being injected directly into their brains within the dominant code. Media scholar Ellen Seiter argues that many intellectuals, educators, and parents assume children are "zombies" with respect to media consumption "who believe that other people's children are already ruined by 'exposure' to" so-called "bad" images in media.[6] Because, in this configuration, there is "bad" and "good" media for children to consume, "good" media provides "good" mediated role models for children. Ultimately, then, clout's convergence with social production results in deliberate consumption of "good" media because of the messages adults believe children can glean from them. Thus, clout and social production are similarly invested in representational politics and consumer citizenship.

Clout, as a concept within this chapter, helps elucidate how Black *Black Panther* fans used the influence and power of their dollars to support the film and to show the Hollywood media industries that Black viewers are a reliable and active consumer segment. As Black visual culture scholar Rebecca Wanzo summarizes, Black consumption "can be an act of resistance in itself, because [. . .] Black shopping and selling are often read as deviant."[7] Deliberate and targeted use of the Black dollar is, within Black communities, understood as a form of activism; it uses, as Black cultural studies scholar bell hooks argues, the act of

Black looking—the very act of Black media consumption—to change the realities of the media industries' relationship to and engagement with Blackness.[8] In short, the use of the Black look is one of the ways Black folks exercise their "civic duty" around media. Elsewhere, I have theorized "civic duty" as a way Black folks use the Black look to suture the personal and the political to attempt to make the act of media consumption serve greater political outcomes.[9] Within civic duty, consumption is not necessarily willful as much as it is a requirement for shoring up specific images of Blackness within media. It is used to both support and withhold support from Black media images based within specific Black taste cultures.

The civic duty Black folks often feel around consuming Black media is not sequestered within specific Black communities. Rather, the relationship between the Black look and the Black dollar is understood and exploited by media industries. Media studies scholar Beretta Smith Shomade persuasively argues that media industries' use of Black-cast media "benefits from and depends upon circulating Black binaries of power and wealth, representation and invisibility."[10] In short, if money is power, then Black folks who hunger for being and feeling "seen" use their dollars and their Black looks to effect industrial change to/for the Hollywood representational landscape. And while being/feeling "seen" in media is important for many Black folks, *Black Panther* also centered that there are particular ways that being/feeling seen is valued: it is through big-budget, Hollywood, "mainstream" fare. Films like *Girls Trip* (2017, dir. Malcolm D. Lee), whose success Colorlines.com writer Sameer Rao says, "rested in large part on a predominantly female and Black audience," are predicated on Black audiences showing "the industry that a Black woman-headlined movie from Black creators can do better than the White-led sci-fi thrillers like *Valerian* [2017, dir. Luc Besson] that tend to become summer blockbusters."[11] And it is not just journalists who write about this aspect of must-see Blackness, or that the compulsion to see Blackness is simply felt; media industries workers, like actress Viola Davis, help to fuel the discourse. About *The Woman King* (2022, dir. Gina Prince-Bythewood), in which she starred, Davis said, "It will just be a moment if people don't come see the movie. Okay? [. . .] Because you're sending a very clear message to a machine called Hollywood . . . Hollywood is interested in green. It just is, it is what I do, so if you don't come see it then you're sending a message that Black women cannot lead the box office globally. You are supporting that narrative."[12] Must-see Blackness is, thus, a discursive formation whose meaning is made contextually by journalists like Rao, industrially via actors like Davis, *and* affectively through audience reception and fan practices. Discursively, then, must-see Blackness is concerned with Black folks using their consumer spending power—or clout—to demonstrate that big-budget Black-cast films can be successful and that courting Black audiences is a money-making rather than a money-losing proposition.

This connection between Blackness and consumer citizenship is certainly not new. Black Americans in the early 20th century were, despite the promises of the Emancipation Proclamation, still being denied the full rights of American citizenship. Historian Robert Weems describes how Black folks' migration for better paying jobs and educational opportunities resulted in their growing stature as consumer citizens. He writes:

> Between 1941 and 1960, white businesses sought to get their "share" of the increasingly lucrative "Negro market" in a number of ways. During this period, major corporations significantly increased their purchasing of advertising space in [B]lack-owned newspapers. Moreover, to supplement their products' enhanced presence in African American periodicals, large U.S. businesses heavily marketed their goods on "Negro-appeal" radio stations. Ironically, while these stations featured music and features of interest to [B]lacks, the vast majority of them were owned by white entrepreneurs.[13]

Alongside the growing recognition of the Black dollar by white businesses and institutions, Black folks simultaneously began recognizing the Black dollar's power to effect change. This is perhaps most famously and successfully demonstrated in the 1955–1956 bus boycott in which Black folks combined activism and consumerism to change public transportation policies in Montgomery, Alabama. Similarly, as media studies scholar Steven D. Classen details, in the early 1960s, Black activists in Clarksdale, Mississippi, routinely "boycotted merchants that had a history of racial discrimination," flexing their dollars to have "a significant economic impact on downtown businesses."[14] In this way, consumerism and visibility became part and parcel of Black folks' configuration of the American Dream.

The successful strategies and tactics of the Black Civil Rights Movement, in which Black folks and their allies came together to fuse the tenets of capitalism and consumerism, were also engaged to effect change around Black representational practices. This politicized use of the Black look can be observed in early television series like *Beulah* (CBS, 1950–1953) and *Amos 'n Andy* (CBS, 1951–1953). Media studies scholar Bambi Haggins details how organizations like the NAACP urged Black folks to withhold their Black look *and* their Black dollars from *Beulah*, *Amos 'n Andy*, and the sponsors supporting the shows (this was in the era of single sponsorship for television programming) as a conduit to register their displeasure with the kinds of images the shows mediated.[15] Additionally, upon the 1978 release of *The Wiz* (1978, dir. Sidney Lumet), some Black journalists used their platforms to encourage Black viewers to see the film. Writer Billy Rowe used his *Call and Post* column to argue that *The Wiz* "is the biggest budgeted film, musical or otherwise, to ever top-cast [B]lack superstars and featured performers. Its box office success would change the face of the silver screen[. . .]. The subtle battle to hold the line and not shakeup the system, through the failure of so costly a [B]lack film, is not beyond the realm of possibility."[16] For his readers, Rowe connects consumption and activism, noting that Hollywood's representational system does not regularly invest money in Black mediation. Writing in 1978, Rowe was keenly aware that Black-cast films had mostly been characterized by the corpus of early 1970s films pejoratively known as Blaxploitation because of their relatively low budgets and, for a time, high box office returns. Even so-called "quality" Black-cast films of the 1970s like *Sounder* (1972, dir. Martin Ritt), *Claudine* (1974, dir. John Berry), and *Uptown Saturday Night* (1974, dir. Sidney Poitier) had small budgets. Twentieth Century Fox spent $1.9 million on *Sounder* and $1.1 million on *Claudine*. The films earned $16.9 million and $6 million in box office receipts respectively. Warner Brothers invested $3 million to make *Uptown Saturday Night* and saw its rentals net $6.7 million. Yet, as I discuss in chapter 3, *The Wiz*'s $23.4 million budget seemed to gesture toward new possibilities for Black-cast films to be imagined as blockbusters. Thus, the importance of flexing Black clout was paramount to *The Wiz* and its industrial and representational potential.

Twenty years after *The Wiz*, Hollywood similarly invested in Black-cast films in the early 1990s, known this time as new Black cinema. But, like their Blaxploitation forebears, these films had small(er) budgets while netting high box office returns. Universal's *Do the Right Thing* (1989, dir. Spike Lee), Columbia's *Boyz n the Hood* (1991, dir. John Singleton), and New Line Cinema's *Set It Off* (1996, dir. F. Gary Gray), made for modest budgets between $6 million and $9 million, grossed $37.3 million, $57.5 million, and $41.6 million, respectively. However, while these films were successful, some of them were simultaneously criticized by Black audiences for their "negative" representations of Blackness. Partly fueled by this dichotomy of "good" and "bad" Black images, in 1998, NPR reported that a group of Black Los Angeles residents "formed a club to support [Black-cast] films with positive themes [. . .] on the first weekend of their release" hoping that "boosting attendance" would encourage production of similar films.[17] Again, Black LA residents (and undoubtedly other Black folks throughout America) used their consumerist Black look as a political tool to signal the kinds of "good" representation they deemed fit for production and distribution. While Black-cast films from 1978 to 1998 often narratively had little in common other than the racial makeup of their principal casts, their Black reception contexts were often similar. Black reception has historically balanced (1) the notion of being/feeling seen, (2) the problematic and slippery categorization of images within a positive/negative binary, and (3) the recognition that representation is filtered through conglomerated media companies whose (mostly white) executives (presumably) make data-based decisions.

Shaped by the relationship between individuals, activism, and looking, Black fan practices around *Black Panther* took on many of the characteristics of consumer citizenship. On the one hand, Black folks were individually invested in *Black Panther* as a text, noting the importance for *them* to see the film because of its "positive" representational attributes. And as I will demonstrate, many Black folks were invested in what the film might mean for Black children and the creation of new Black role models (or what I call Black social production). On the other hand, as communication scholar Sarah Banet Weiser argues about consumer citizenship generally, Black *Black Panther* fans were also "community-minded and selfless. In this way, the community-minded individual is still created, but the community itself is part of a brand."[18] Put another way, Black *Black Panther* fans consumed *Black Panther* "for the culture," imagining what the film's success could mean for the future of Black-cast film production.

Since 2010, Black folks had been the subject of reports that fashioned them as consumer citizens through their spending power. American studies scholar Arlene Davila argues that markets are not naturally occurring, but are instead created through a series of marketing industry moves.[19] While it is true that media industries catered to Black audiences prior to the 21st century, the ways Black folks understood their spending power and advertisers' and media industries' interest in that spending power coalesced in this period. Beginning in 2010, Nielsen began producing reports on Black consumers and their spending habits. Media historian Eleanor Patterson details how the broadcast network ABC used this (re)creation of the Black market to develop multicultural programming that would attract both Black (often female) viewers *and* more lucrative white (often also women) viewers. Pointing to the network's 2014 social media campaign #TGIT (Thank God It's Thursday), Patterson argues that ABC's turn to diversity "appeared not only in response to public outcry demanding diversity but also as a reaction to the emergence of new gendered and racialized market research" in media industries. Similarly, in fall 2014, Marvel announced *Black Panther* and *Captain Marvel* as part of their upcoming slate of films. Deadline.com reported the news, suggesting that the two films would "bring diversity to [the studio's] superhero slate," centering that diversity had become a part of the media industries' brand strategy.[20] Armed with their dollars and the knowledge that their spending power, which according to the 2018 Nielsen report was $1.3 trillion, could effect change, Black *Black Panther* fans sought to show up and show out for the first Black-cast blockbuster of the 21st century.

Welcome to Wakanda: A Black Blockbuster Meets Black Style

Although *Black Panther* had a primarily Black cast, its enormous budget meant that the film could not be construed as one that specifically hailed Black audiences and fans. The sheer size of the film's budget and its star-studded cast made it what media industries scholar Justin Wyatt defines as a blockbuster: those films that have "*more* stars, *higher* budget, [and a] *more* exciting story."[21] As I have argued elsewhere, Black spectators and fans "were considered surplus to the target Marvel audience. For example, while undoubtedly some Black folks were watching, the film's first trailer aired during the NBA Finals. And the announcement of the film's ticket presale was somewhat similarly announced in a national ad during the College Football Playoff National Championship on January 8, 2018."[22] But even as Black folks were surplus to the main audience *Black Panther* seemingly sought, the power of Black representation and the precarity of Black image production meant that *Black Panther*'s size and scope activated some of the same anxieties for Black moviegoers that *The Wiz* had 40 years prior: Black folks felt a sense of must-see Blackness around the film as well as the need to evangelize in order to encourage other Black moviegoers to also see the film.[23] This impulse is often dissociated from the film being categorically "good." Rather, it is located within an understanding of the media industry's relationship with Black-cast content. Like Hollywood turned away from Black-cast content in the wake of *The Wiz* failing to recoup its budget in its initial US theatrical run (opting instead to invest in the interracial buddy comedy), and Fox, UPN, and the WB turned away from Black-cast sitcoms when whiter and wealthier audiences were available and interested, this chapter details how Black *Black Panther* fans understood (or imagined they understood) the stakes of the film's initial theatrical release.

Black Panther was not "just" a blockbuster—it felt like a *Black* blockbuster. As Black *Black Panther* fan Devon, 46, from Philadelphia, details:

> I feel like *Black Panther* was almost made in a way so that white people have to experience race the way Black people wish they experienced race. Which is, like, seeing it, but also acknowledging that there are other dimensions to a person besides it. So, it's not colorblindness, right? [. . .] It's not, like, oh, the cast could have been white, or Asian, or anything. It was just a good movie. No. This is a Black movie. These are Black people. See them? See them in their full Blackness, and now let's go.

Unlike the logics that typically accompany large-budget Black-cast films (and most Black-cast TV series content), Devon hypothesizes that there was less apprehension around Blackness with *Black Panther*. While colorblind casting had explicitly come into fashion in both television (Shonda Rhimes's production company Shondaland) and Broadway (Lin-Manuel

Miranda's *Hamilton*), Devon suggests these logics were not principally at play in *Black Panther*. Instead, she forwards that *Black Panther* centered a Black cultural specificity that "insists that rather than the characters 'happening to be Black,' it is more authentic and resonant if they are written as they are—with all the experiences, histories, and cultures that are tied to that identity marker."[24] For Devon, *Black Panther* felt different from other Black-cast films in that while Marvel and Disney carefully considered casting and director selections with an eye toward marketability and wider and whiter audience appeal, the standard "race-based judgments that constrain movies with Black actors and directors and reward movies with white actors and directors based on biased perceptions of box-office potential" seemed less central than they are with "regular" Black-cast films.[25] In other words, *Black Panther* certainly felt different with respect to its stars, budget, and story, but also in the relationship between those factors and the industrial calculus that often attempts to mitigate Blackness for white audiences. *Black Panther felt* Black and as such Black fans took up the text as resonant for/to Black culture.

But it was not "just" seeing the film; for some Black people, *Black Panther* was an event. *Black Panther* activated Black fandom practices often dissociated from Black-cast film—namely, the notion of getting dressed to attend the film. On the one hand, companies like Black-owned clothing retailer Diyanu encouraged Black *Black Panther* fans to visit their website to plan their film-going outfits. That sartorial choices should be considered for a visit to the multiplex gestured toward the import of *Black Panther* as a cultural event for which the stakes were high. Similarly, a Facebook user encouraged Black people to "stop stressing over whether or not your outfit is too extra for *Black Panther*. Have fun. Ride in on a fuckin [sic] zebra." In other words, Black folks were encouraged to connect the importance of *Black Panther* to Black media production with their clothing. *Black Panther* was deemed special because its high budget meant that its failure could vanquish high-budget Black-cast film production. As such, Black *Black Panther* fans were encouraged to connect that specialness to their attire. Angelica, 48, from Phoenix, designed an outfit to wear to see the film to underscore the connective tissue between the film's importance to Black culture and Black style.

This chapter asks why Black fans chose to see *Black Panther* and to see it in movie theaters during its initial theatrical release. As an

Figure 2.1. Fashion company Diyanu's Facebook ad to promote their clothing for *Black Panther* screenings.

intermediary question, this chapter asks why *Black Panther* was important to Black fans. I ask these two questions in part to explore how and why no similar must-see Blackness emerged around Black-cast "quality" films also released in 2018 like *If Beale Street Could Talk* (2018, dir. Barry Jenkins) or *BlacKkKlansman* (2018, dir. Spike Lee), or four years later for *Black Panther: Wakanda Forever* (*Wakanda Forever*) (2022, dir. Ryan Coogler). This chapter uses interviews with 20 self-professed Black *Black Panther* fans recruited via Facebook and Twitter

Figure 2.2. Facebook post encouraging Black people to have fun with their outfits for *Black Panther* screenings.

to argue that Black fans used their clout to ensure *Black Panther*'s commercial success. And, ultimately, their Black fandom practices are imbricated in the politics of media industries because they attempt to use their Black dollars to effect industrial change.

The 20 Black *Black Panther* fans I interviewed for this chapter help theorize clout (see sidebar for full biographical details). Through their discussions of Black futurity, must-see Blackness, and consumerism, these Black fans inherently understand their Black look as a conduit to shift the cultural, industrial, and representational politics of mediated Blackness. These one-on-one interviews took place in February 2018 and lasted between 45 and 75 minutes each (see the appendix for the questions that guided the interviews). To participate in this project, these Black people needed to identify themselves as Black fans of the film *Black Panther* and had seen the film at least once prior to our conversation. These Black fans' in-depth, one-on-one interviews illuminate how the Black look is not "just" about looking, but about using their fandom to activate their look for broader Black aims.

Figure 2.3. Angelica in her *Black Panther*–inspired outfit. Photo used with permission.

BLACK BLACK PANTHER FANS

Angelica is a married woman who lives in Phoenix, Arizona. A self-described comic book fan, Angelica says she has "known about Black Panther for a long time." She continues, "I've seen the new iterations of the story that have come out with Roxanne Gay and Ta-Nehisi Coates [as authors], so like two years ago when I found out that they were thinking about doing a movie, I'm like, 'I have to see it. I have to see it.' [...] So, I really ignored the hype and tried to not focus on the hype because if a movie is hyped up too much, I usually won't see it because it's usually super disappointing." Angelica is heterosexual and was born in 1975.

Anson was born in 1975 and is an attorney who currently lives in upstate New York. He identifies as heterosexual and is a divorced father. Anson says, "I enjoy the superhero flicks, but I've never been huge into comics. I've always been on the periphery [...] but for me, the draw of [*Black Panther*] as I learned more about it, it was like, 'Man this is something by and for Black people that looks like a really good story.' The fact that it was put out by Marvel wasn't a primary motivation for me, but it certainly didn't hurt."

Born in 1991, **Arienne** was excited when she saw the first *Black Panther* trailer "because . . . well, first, it's basically all Black folks, which is . . . That never happens unless it's a movie specifically about racism or something like. [But *Black Panther* is] a superhero movie. There's been Black superheroes, but it's not been situations where *everybody* in the cast is Black. And so, I thought that was really exciting. [. . .] And then seeing other people get excited about it, too. Like, people who normally don't care that much about superhero movies or don't really watch them too much. Watching people like that get hyped up and excited also made me more excited."

Ashley is single, lives in Chicago, and was born in 1984. She says, "I'm not into action films [. . .] I'm not familiar with comic books at all. So, I typically don't go to [those kinds of films . . .]. I typically don't go see action or superhero movies. Especially by Marvel . . . Marvel I'm totally unfamiliar with." But Ashley saw *Black Panther* because "the more I recognized the power of a Black cast, the power of it being a superhero film and considering not only who in front of the camera, but now that I'm older, I pay a bit more attention to who's behind the camera as well. So, when I learned about who the costume designers were, who was doing writing, and all those things in the background, the people we don't necessarily see, I was intrigued because that also means a bit more to me than something that might've been produced by someone who doesn't look like the characters on the screen."

Born and raised in Detroit, **Channon** is a married woman who was born in 1975. A former history teacher, Channon first started reading the history of when and why the Black Panther comic was created. She says, "From there, I started reading about Luke Cage and the Falcon to kind of see how Stan Lee came up with some of these characters at a time when you would think he wouldn't necessarily market to African Americans." Channon became particularly excited about the *Black Panther* movie through *Captain America: Civil War* (2016, dir. Anthony Russo and Joe Russo), a film whose plot partly includes a glimpse of Wakanda. "So, it was exciting to see that they're finally going to take us into another world to get some backstory on [T'challa . . .] and Marvel doesn't do that with every character. So that's when I first got excited about *Black Panther*."

A self-described "movie head," **Clarence** identifies as heterosexual and was born in 1993. The Detroit resident says, "If [a film is] a Marvel movie, a Disney movie, a Star Wars movie or a superhero movie in general, I'm probably going to go see it." Clarence vividly remembers when *Black Panther* was announced as a Marvel Cinematic Universe film. He says, "I know there had been rumors like, 'Hey, Marvel. When you going to make a *Black Panther* movie?' Kevin Feige [president of Marvel] would be like, 'Well, it's going to come eventually. Don't worry.'" He adds that his first response to seeing T'Challa appear in *Civil War* was, "'Oh, that guy is awesome!' I kind of already knew that his movie was going to come out. I just didn't know who was playing him or anything like that until *Civil War*."

Devon, a heterosexual, divorced woman who lives in Philadelphia, selects films to see in movie theaters by "sort of a combination of news coverage, which I'll see on social media. Maybe I see an advertisement. Because I don't go to a lot of movies, I don't see a lot of previews. So, I tend to, like, decide based on, oh . . . I hear a story about this is happening, and I get interested in the story." The last movie Devon, born in 1977, saw in a theater before *Black Panther* was *I, Tonya* (2017, dir. Craig Gillespie). "There was a lot of discussion about Tonya Harding, and that kind of stuff, so I got interested and I went to see that." The "hype" around *Black Panther* is partly what convinced Devon to see *Black Panther* on opening weekend.

Eric was born in 1974, currently lives in Austin, Texas, and identifies as heterosexual. He decided to see *Black Panther* for three reasons: "So, I follow movies, first of all. Secondly, like I said I'm a comic nerd, so I watch out for what's going on. Third of all, I'm from Oakland and Ryan Coogler is from Oakland, so I kind of check to see if there is something going on in my town or something about Oakland. I'm all on board with that too."

At the time of our interview, **Felix**, a heterosexual man, lived in Miami. Born in 1986, Felix describes himself as a "huge, huge comic book fan." As a Black man and a comic book fan, Felix says, "Growing up, after *Spawn* [1997, dir. Mark A. Z. Dippé] came out, even though he was severely disfigured for the entire film, that character, Al Simmons, is an African American male! I was like, 'I don't get to see Black superheroes often. I'll take even the disfigured Black character because I know he's Black.' When I heard *Blade* [1998, dir. Stephen Norrington] was coming out, again, I was like, 'No way they're gonna make a Blade movie.' Then, when it came out, I was like, 'Okay, maybe this might be the start of something, maybe we might get high-quality comic book films with Black superheroes going forward.'" He says when Feige announced the *Black Panther* film and said, "'It's gonna have 97 percent Black people,' I was like, you guys are really willing to dedicate between 80 million to 120 million to do a film with a 97 percent African American cast?"

Helius was born in 1976 and currently lives in New York. He identifies as heterosexual and typically goes to the movies "like every three months, six months." The thing that structures when Helius pays to go see a movie in a theater is whether it has some kind of "significance or I'm pretty sure [it] will be really good. Because you spend a lot of money for food and for the ticket itself and having to deal with all the other headaches of people talking and sticky floors. So, I'd rather see it at home because the technology caught up where you can have a large TV and surround sound. But when you have movies like *Black Panther* or any other ones that you know are going to be good, I take my time and go and see it."

Keith was born in 1981, is heterosexual, and lives in Austin. He does not tend to pay attention to film paratexts because he likes "being fresh" when he sees a film. However, he says, "I did watch the trailer [for *Black Panther*] that came on during the college football playoffs, so I watched that and it looked great and I was like, 'You know, I don't want to see anymore.'" Before seeing the film, he listened "to the *Black Panther* soundtrack that Kendrick put out" and read the comic book to understand the *Black Panther* universe. "So I just read a little bit about the origin, how it was the first recurring role for Black superheroes. So I kind of got a little bit of the history, not a deep dive by any stretch. It was really just understanding the universe, it was not about trying to understand anything necessarily about the movie."

Kina lives in St. Petersburg, Florida, and was born in 1976. She is a heterosexual, single woman who does not often go to the theater to see movies because she does not "really like crowds." She goes to the movie theater "maybe once in three to six months" and decides on movies to see there based on "if I see the trailer and it gets me really excited." In addition, Kina will see a movie in theaters "if it seems to have a story that connects with me or a cast I really like[. . . .] I also see movies that have a message that I really want to see and would like movie studios to put more out there, and I feel like my going will contribute to the cause, then I would go and support it, because, you know, money speaks."

Kristal is a pansexual woman born in 1986 and who currently resides in Tampa. Kristal says going to a movie theater to see films is difficult because she has two contract jobs and is "busy six days a week." She continues, "getting out to the movies—even just like once a month—can be a lot for [my husband and I] especially since it's getting so expensive. But I've seen *Black Panther* twice this month already." Kristal grew up watching and being a fan of superhero movies and remembers that when she was a seven-year-old, "My Dad took me to see *Spawn*."

Lynn has "become invested in a couple of the franchises, since Hollywood has gotten so good about that kind of entertainment. Purely for the joy of entertainment, I like the Marvel franchise." Born in 1961, Lynn lives in Austin and identifies as a pansexual woman. She says, "growing up I was not into Marvel comics or even DC comics to a huge extent. I would read comics in the newspaper, but I wouldn't get tons of comic books. All of this is kind of new to me and I'm not invested in whether or not the movie is true to the comic. I was there for the sheer joy and the entertainment of it, but I think with *Black Panther*, it has taken on a life of its own in terms of representation."

Born in 1990, **Melanie** first heard about *Black Panther* on social media. She says, "I think some famous person I follow mentioned it. And then the whispers started that Rank Shoogloo would be directing. And then I saw the poster. It was a rough draft—I think it was a fan made poster of all these people that were supposedly going to be in the film. And that's when I knew, oh this is serious." Melanie, a heterosexual woman who lives in Natchez, Mississippi, says she was excited about *Black Panther* because "it was all Black. I'm rooting for everyone Black."

Nichole was excited about *Black Panther* for a few reasons. "The first thing... just the excitement of this Black superhero getting his *own* movie because we're not totally represented in this fashion[....] Some [Black-cast movies] have really good stories and really good acting, but then you get some of them where it's so stereotypical or so low brow or, just... you gotta play the husband, you gotta play the drug dealer, you gotta play the sidekick, you gotta play the goofball. It's never really anything of substance as far as I'm concerned." Born in 1973 and currently residing in Oakland, California, Nichole says she got even more excited "once they signed Ryan Coogler on to direct [*Black Panther*]. I'm a huge fan of his. I can't tell you how many times I've watched *Creed* and *Fruitvale Station*, and him being from Oakland, that was another source of excitement for me. It's great for me to see a young African American man doing things but also maintaining his roots and his authenticity in the person that he is." The heterosexual woman says, "Lastly, I'm so happy about the cast, they're just gorgeous! When I found out that Chadwick Boseman was gonna, they're gonna give him his own full-length movie, I was like, 'Yes, Lord! Thank you!'"

Nikki, a lesbian born in 1971, believes "Marvel makes the far superior product over DC," even as she doesn't "rush out to the theaters to see Marvel." She says, "I'll usually wait to experience that in the comfort of my home." The Atlanta resident says, "I knew a little bit about the *Black Panther* comics, but it was not a whole lot, and it was really when [Coogler] got attached that I was like, 'Alright. Awesome. Let's do this!'"

Rodney was born in 1954 and remembers "the *Blade* Trilogies and [how] his race wasn't an issue . . . we knew that Blade was Black, but it didn't matter as far as his ethnicity. But *Black Panther*, that's a whole different thing, especially in our current climate and how we're challenged with our existence as Black folk and how people perceive us. It makes a big difference to us to see this movie come out *now* so, it holds much bigger value." The heterosexual Las Vegas resident suggests that *Blade* and *Black Panther* are fundamentally different in their approaches to Blackness and that the latter is less engaged with colorblindness. He says, "Blade was one of the first black superheroes. Blade is a black man who killed vampires. The storyline behind Blade was never really based on him being a *Black* man killing vampires. It was Blade, a *vampire* slayer. And the writers didn't make his race key to the storyline, even though it was obvious he's a black guy. With *Black Panther*, his Blackness made a big difference. It was key to the storyline."

Stephanie was born in 1975 and lives in Ypsilanti, Michigan, a suburb of Detroit. She identifies as a lesbian and typically will see Black-cast films during their theatrical runs "just to support—with the exception of Tyler Perry movies. I don't do those [. . .]. But I try to support." Stephanie's says she supports Black-cast films in their theatrical runs because bootlegs of those films "don't support the cast, they don't support the movie. That doesn't help a movie's success, as far as the box office is concerned, to buy a bootleg at the barber shop."

Born in Detroit, but currently living in Los Angeles, **Tara** was born in 1974. Tara and her husband were both excited about *Black Panther* but for slightly different reasons. She says, "I had been following Ryan Coogler's career for a little bit. [My husband] generally follows superhero news. I think we both saw that [Coogler] was directing it and thought 'Oh, my god! That's kind of a game changer.' You know what I mean? The fact that it was a Black director directing a Black character. And then as it progressed, there were more Black people associated with it and we just kept getting more and more excited about it. I didn't even see a trailer, but I was still super, super interested and excited about it."

Opening the Black Wallet:
Black Panther = Black Box Office Gold

Black Panther performed massively when it opened on February 16, 2018, garnering $192 million in its first weekend—setting a record for Marvel's highest first weekend gross. Black folks' reliance on the logics of scarcity and belief in their industrial clout as an audience segment meant that Black folks supported *Black Panther* in droves. Writer Tom Huddleston, Jr., notes that, on average, Black folks comprise only 15 percent of movie audiences. However, as he reported for Fortune.com, Black folks made up 37 percent of *Black Panther*'s audience on its opening weekend.[26] In short, Black folks contributed $71 million of *Black Panther*'s first weekend haul, demonstrating their clout to help make the film a success.

And while Black audiences contributed more than one-third of the film's first weekend haul, Disney understood that Black audiences could not make the film as successful as they wanted it to be. As such, *Black Panther* was, I argue, three films in one: a Marvel film for white superhero film fans, a Black-cast film for a "general" Black audience, and a Black-cast Marvel film for Black comic book/superhero fans. As film and media studies scholar Racquel Gates argues with respect to *Coming to America* (1988, dir. John Landis), some Black-cast films exemplify a cinematic double consciousness in which the same film functions as a film for white viewers and a different film for Black viewers.[27] I expand Gates's theorization here to suggest that *Black Panther* deliberately hailed three audiences simultaneously to result in a Venn diagram in which Marvel's core white comic book film audience, Black folks wanting to see a Black-cast film with a high budget, and Black folks seeing a Black-cast superhero film converged to ensure box office success. Black fans like Angelica, 48, of Phoenix, underscore this cinematic polysemy. She says, "Both times I saw the movie with a predominantly white audience. And the parts that hit me, they totally missed. 'Cause they're not coming for that. So, it needed to be [mainstream . . .] to be successful [. . .] And it's not a social commentary film. And you can't make it profitable by putting these huge messages and leaving people wanting." Angelica underscores her reading of *Black Panther* as a film that can be understood by mainstream (read: white) audiences and one that holds deeper intertextual meaning for Black audiences because of the ways it mediates Black culture. But more importantly, she centers an understanding of the calculus that brings big-budget Black-cast films to market. And in a good example of intertextuality, in which some of the references and topics may go unnoticed by certain segments of an audience, Angelica underscores how the deeper meanings that resonated with her did not affect how audiences outside her subject position understood and enjoyed the film. Rodney, 69, of Las Vegas, adds:

> if anything, I would say [*Black Panther*] should tell a lot of the white folk who think they can't relate to Black movies, this should give them the understanding of knowing how we, as Black folk, when we go to see movies, we're very used to seeing lack of representation of us. [. . .] So, now that we have this movie that moves the needle, it shows that, hey, you really can see more of our movies. And guess what white folks or anyone who's not Black? You should wanna see [Black-cast movies] too. I truly believe that we should see [*Black Panther*] as a mainstream movie with Black folks in it.

Partly, then, Black fans use their Black look (and Black *Black Panther* fans' looking for the culture) to shift how the sign of Blackness is industrially understood by white executives with the power to greenlight Black-cast projects. In addition, *Black Panther* signals, for Black fans, how white decoding practices of Black-cast media should shift. Concomitantly, Rodney suggests that Blackness, in all its particularity, can also be universal and appeal to non-Black audiences.

Because the Black look is concerned with being an agent for Black change, *Black Panther* was not a film Black folks wanted to see via bootleg versions sold in Black beauty and barber shops or by street vendors in areas heavily populated and patronized by Black folks like Harlem's 125th Street. Rather, Black folks needed to see the film in a movie theater. And they needed to see it when their Black look would count: on opening weekend. Black *Black Panther* fans like Anson, 48, upstate New York, believe "opening weekend [is] a great indicator of how the film is going to do, how much money it's going to make." Anson centers how opening weekend allows studios like Marvel to project a film's financial future, and as such, he uses his Black look to signal that more Black-cast films like *Black Panther* should be produced. Kina, 42, St. Petersburg, Florida, says seeing the film on its opening weekend "was important because that's the excuse that I feel we're always given when we're getting told the same stories on the screen. [. . .] 'Well, it's not going to sell overseas,' or 'Not everybody is going to come see it.' Money talks. So, I felt that it was really important to see it [on opening weekend]." Kina, like Anson, correlates her personal spending to Hollywood's spending on Black-cast films believing that by helping to produce stellar box office receipts, the media industries will continue to seek the Black dollar through similar "high quality" projects. Channon, 48, Ypsilanti, Michigan, and her husband also saw the film on opening weekend "just to contribute to the [box office] numbers." Lynn, 62, Austin, Texas, says, "It's rare for me to go see a movie more than once in a movie theater on opening weekend, but I'm really invested in making sure that this movie is as popular and successful as I can." Helius, 47, New York City, similarly saw *Black Panther* twice on opening weekend—once on Friday and once on Saturday "to support the film financially. It's important when you have really good Black films that come out, that you support it [. . .]. I don't usually see films opening day because it's a mad house [. . . but] I just had to be part of [*Black Panther*], man, I wanted to be there opening night." Lynn and Helius center that they rarely see films on opening weekend, and as such, center the specialness of *Black Panther* and the ways that the film's distinction as a Black-cast blockbuster garnered their support for the film on opening weekend because of their investment in its success. In this way, Black fans' consumption of *Black Panther* is structured around ensuring a healthy future for Black-cast film production. Black *Black Panther* fans, then, are "good" Black consumer citizens in tethering their desire for "good" Black film representation to the ways they spend their discretionary income.

Melanie adds that by seeing the film on opening weekend she "was trying to break box office records, not just me singularly, but I was trying to see if we'd beat out the other superhero movies. [. . .] Hollywood is very slow to change. They say, 'Oh diversity!' But they don't really actually do diversity. [. . .] Disney put in an effort and the camp—the whole [*Black Panther*] crew was Black. And that is not really common within the industry. They don't give that much space to us." Melanie invokes the communal Black "we" in discussing the effort to make *Black Panther* successful. In her desire for the film to "beat out" the box office results of other Marvel films, she signals her belief in the ways data generally, and data about Black patronage for *Black Panther* specifically, might shift industrial hypotheses about Black-cast content and Black audiences. These logics collectively shaped Anson, Helius, Channon, Lynn, and Melanie's desire to be "part of that massive showing of support" for *Black Panther* on its opening weekend. In each instance, these Black fans demonstrate how they understood both the scarcity of high-budget Black-cast film production and the fleeting nature with which the media industries create content for Black audiences. And while *Black Panther* made Blackness visible on-screen, Black *Black Panther* fans wanted to make themselves visible off-screen to media industries decision-makers who hold the power to reflect their lives back to them through film and television.

In short, Black folks' desire to see *Black Panther* is rooted in the activism of the Black look. Arienne, 32, of College Park, Pennsylvania, rhetorically asks, "Can an all-Black cast superhero movie succeed?" before answering, "By all accounts, absolutely. So, those sort of outdated questions have clearly been answered. When you have a good cast, when you have good characters . . . And honestly, when you have Marvel branding behind it, these movies can do really well. And so, my hope would be that people will start pushing the envelope and giving us more of these movies to where it's not a once-in-a-lifetime thing." Arienne's rhetorical question about the viability of Black-cast superhero films centers notions about how, where, and why mainstream media industries invest in projects with Black casts. At the same time, she configures her (and Black folks', writ large) consumption of *Black Panther* within the logics of good consumer citizenship. Thus, if she (and other Black folks) showed up to see *Black Panther* like good consumer citizens, the Hollywood media industries should reward that consumer citizenship by greenlighting more fare in the same vein.

Helius centers the scarcity of Black-cast media production by hypothesizing that if *Black Panther* didn't "do well, we won't see another *Black Panther* or [the media industries] won't fully invest in it the second time around and not just for *Black Panther* but for *all* Black films. Like if we don't go out and see it [. . .] then it will give an excuse to Hollywood saying, 'Ah, you see, Black films don't do well.'" In other words, Black *Black Panther* fans understand the ways the present connects to the future. As I have argued elsewhere, Black folks "understand that any singular Black failure industrially represents the limits of all Black-cast media content [. . .] Industrial understandings of Black-cast film production is univocal: any Black-cast film must be a financial success, or it will vanquish the idea of making others like it."[28] Framed by scarcity and what media scholar Tim Havens calls industry logic, Helius demonstrates an awareness that conversations around mediated Blackness are structured by (usually white) executives who assume that Black-cast media content is particular to Black audiences and rarely assumed to have universal appeal.[29] In the final analysis, Black *Black Panther* fans placed extraordinary importance on the film's opening weekend performance as a way to ensure Black cinematic futurity and to demonstrate their clout as a consumer segment that should be aggressively courted by the media industries.

For the Culture: Black Fandom, Industry Logics, and Black Futurity

For many Black people, representation is not *just* representation. Rather, the Black act of consuming media employs a double consciousness: it is structured by an awareness of images and how they can be read by Black folks; concomitantly, the Black look assumes that the production of Black images is tethered to Black futurity in a Hollywood industry structured by whiteness and racism. And Black consumption is simultaneously cognizant of the inner workings of capitalism on the content they consume as they look toward the future of Black-cast media production. Black cultural theorist Kara Keeling notes the necessity of interrogating the "four constitutive elements of Afrofuturism—imagination, technology, the future, and liberation—within the context of finance capital's stances toward (and investments in) the future."[30] Put another way, Black *Black Panther* fans do not disentangle the notion that the film is a (by)product of racialized capitalist systems. Eric, 49, Austin, demonstrates an understanding of this confluence. He says:

> I've heard all these little ramblings and rumblings about its still being a Disney movie [. . .] but the reality of it is if I'm allowed to put my message out and it's my message and my vision then I don't have so much of a problem with [Disney backing the film]. That's where the representation is important. What I'm saying is if you have a company that wants you to put a message that is not representative of who you are and has its own agenda then that's when it's like we need to do our own thing[. . . .] But, you know, if you're given the opportunity to portray who you are, I don't care who is backing it. We all have our own goals, obviously [Disney's] goal is to make money and the movie made almost a half a billion dollars so they got their wish and [Coogler's] goal was to put out a movie that represented who and what he thought should be represented. We got our wish.

Eric details the calculus he engages to elevate *Black Panther*. It is not simply that the film had Black talent behind the camera, but Black talent who demonstrated a keen understanding of Black culture. Eric seemingly suggests that within his idea of films that represent Black culture, he subscribes to the axiom that not all kinfolk are skinfolk. Or put another way, Eric suggests that having Black creatives behind a film does not automatically make it an "authentic" representation of Blackness and Black culture. Rather, it is the *right* Black folks who can mediate a version of Black culture that resonates with Black audiences. For Tara, 49, Los Angeles, the resonance of *Black Panther* was partially found in the ways it made Blackness central. She says, "I thought that on so many different levels [*Black Panther*] was a game changer because the white people were not crucial to the story. [. . .] So, it kind of had nothing to do with white people for me, in general. [. . . Blackness] was the A story. I was worried about creating this fictional African country where I was like, who's gonna have what accent? Like what's gonna happen? I thought that they did a really good job of blending a lot of different Black cultures." Tara observes that *Black Panther* centered Blackness and did so while narratively sidelining whiteness. At the same time, in centering Blackness, *Black Panther* made space for diasporic Blackness recognizing that there is not one whole Africa, or one monolithic Black "community," but one made up of many kinds of Blackness that run the spectrum of politics, skin tone, and ideology. Together, Eric and Tara demonstrate how the Black look, and Black fandom by extension, is undergirded by a sense that Black folks are, to turn the phrase, looking for the culture. The notion of doing something for the culture suggests that activities like *Black Panther* consumption have an "additional perceived value" outside of just doing the activity for the pleasure of it.[31] That is, "doing it for the culture" is built on the surplusness of the Black look. It is, as Black cultural theorist bell hooks suggests, not simply about the act of looking; rather it centers how the Black look is deployed to change industrial and representational practices.[32] This section reveals Black *Black Panther* fans' deployment of the Black look to do it for the culture.

Ashley, 39, Chicago, suggests that her choice to see a film in a theater versus waiting for it to premiere on a streaming platform is related to the cast. She says, "I'll go see [a movie in a theater] if it's a film with a predominantly African American cast . . . If I feel that I can be supported by the culture [. . .] And then it'll be like Will Smith in *Ali*? We gotta go support it because that's—how often do we get that, right?" Kristal, 37, Tampa, adds that she, too, saw *Black Panther* for the culture. "There was a part of me that felt like, 'You know what? Even if [*Black Panther*] is bad, we still need to go and support it and show Disney that we want more and show Disney and Marvel that this is what we want." Black folks' use of their look is tied to economic logics—the power of the Black dollar is understood as the remedy for Black cinematic scarcity. Kristal notes that *Black Panther*'s import lies not necessarily within an aesthetic valuation of the film (a topic to which I return in chapter 3 about *The Wiz*), but in its size and scope. This deployment of the Black dollar is bound within must-see Blackness in its activation of consumer citizenship's connection to the American Dream. Black consumer citizenship is not necessarily about the individual Black person "making it" but is concerned with Blackness as a collective "making it." Thus, part of "doing it for the culture" involves, as Issa Rae said on the 2017 Emmy red carpet, "rooting for everybody Black" by turning *Black Panther* from just a Black-cast film to one that activates Black fans' must-see Blackness.

In gesturing toward a Black mediated future, Kina, 42, of St. Petersburg, Florida, introduces the slippery notion of "quality" into a discussion of *Black Panther*'s importance around consumption. She says she saw *Black Panther* because "it's something different from what we're normally shown with a predominantly Black cast and the fact that [*Black Panther*] has a major movie studio backing it. So, I felt like, okay, so now it's going to have a high budget, so it will be high quality, and I wanted to see that, and I wanted to support that." *Black Panther*'s difference for Black fandom is situated within its discursively higher quality vis-à-vis other Black-cast films. As media scholars Elana Levine and Michael Newman argue, American media discourse works in a binary opposition that defines the category of "quality" not necessarily by what it is, but by what it is not.[33] In other words, Kina connects *Black Panther* to quality through its expense (an estimated $200 million budget), its connection to an already legitimated studio (Disney), and its elevation above "regular" Black-cast films.

In short, Black *Black Panther* fans have a keen awareness of how the sign of Blackness moves within the culture industries. Nichole, 50, Oakland, California, says in interviews media industries workers always say:

> people of color don't go to the movies, and Black movies don't do well because Black people don't go to the movies. And they never wanna buy the scripts, they never wanna produce the movies because, in their opinion, Black people don't go to the movies and the movies aren't gonna do well. Well, we know that's not necessarily true because we've all gone to Black movies when they've been sold out and when the buzz and anticipation is relatively high. We also know that Hollywood doesn't put a lot behind our movies. I don't think Marvel necessarily did it [with *Black Panther*] because it was a Black movie; they did it because it was a superhero movie, and they know that their superhero movies do well.

Looking toward the future of Black Hollywood production fuels Black consumption of *Black Panther*. Black *Black Panther* fans like Nichole are fighting for not just visibility but recognition from the media industries. They believe that by consuming Black-cast media, and making a loud display of that consumption, the media industries will both recognize the importance of Black audiences *and* Black-cast media production by supporting more projects. Extending this connection between consumption and futurity, Ashley, 39, Chicago, underscores that *Black Panther* consumption is important because it could open doors for the future of Black media production. She says, "I would like for [*Black Panther*–type films] to be the norm in Hollywood. I would like for this film to kick open the door to more representation. Better representation, and more inclusive representation." Not only does Ashley want more Black media production, but it should hew on the side on "better" representation, which, of course, is subjective, but means something to/for Ashley. She says she considers *Black Panther* a film with "better" representation—she "was happy the protagonist's love interest was not light-skinned, and that caused a bit of a stir given [my own light skin]. I had a moment there where you see Chadwick [T'Challa] and Lupita [Nakia] I was like, 'Wow, when was the last time I saw a dark-skinned Black man [pursuing] a dark-skinned Black woman?'" Ashley's concern about representation is partly rooted in her desire for images that depart from tropes about Black love and darker-skinned Black women's attractiveness and romantic desirability. And importantly, she is willing to use her clout to signal her support of particular kinds of Black representation and Black love.

In thinking about the future of Black cinema, Felix, 37, Miami, says, now that the media industries are interested in Black films and Black audiences:

> you just have to pray that you don't have a situation where all these executives are like, "Well, we know that Black people can spend money. Let's find some Black projects to throw money at." Then, they'll give them the initial green light and you'll be like, "Great." Then, they'll be like, "Oh, this film seems awfully Black. Well, let's add in a white love interest and let's do this." [. . .] But, instead of thinking, "Let's go find a new African American director, or writer, or just people of color in general." You now have a situation where they may have just been like, "Yeah, we could do that, or we could just try and throw more money at Coogler to make him drop whatever project he's working on to work for us. We could throw more money at Jordan Peele; we could throw more money at [Ava] DuVernay."

Felix demonstrates an understanding of how media industries have historically interacted with Black audiences and Black content. He gestures toward how Hollywood exercises willful amnesia around the viability and visibility of Black audiences. For Felix, it is as if, with *Black Panther*, suddenly Black audiences materialized as a consumer segment. And in this current iteration, Felix hopes the industry refrains from greenlighting projects simply because of the industrial interest in Black audiences (and Black dollars). He similarly understands that via this industrial amnesia, Blackness might very well be extracted from Black-cast content and, instead, added to white/multicultural content where Blackness can add a little bit of spice "that can liven up the dull dish that is mainstream white culture" for whiter and industrially more desirable audiences.[34] At the same time, he understands (and fears) the media industries' risk averseness in which known talent, known properties, and known products help to mitigate the volatile relationship between rising production costs and ever-changing audience tastes resulting in not necessarily opportunities for Black filmmakers, but new opportunities for established and "industry-tested" filmmakers like Coogler, Jordan Peele, and Ava DuVernay.[35] Felix uses his clout to "show Hollywood" that Black audiences are viable, but he is wary of the ways media industries will (mis)use that clout. Put simply, Felix and Black *Black Panther* fans are interested in more Black-cast Hollywood productions but are also interested in Hollywood granting more (and different) Black talent a seat at its table.

Black Clout and Black Futures in the Looking Glass

Black Panther was almost immediately structured as a film that Black children should see. The importance of the film, and of consuming it in theaters, was laid bare in a fourth season episode of *Blackish* (ABC, 2014–2022). Before a commercial break, the series created a special interstitial to publicize *Black Panther*, which was produced by Marvel—one of ABC's sister companies in the Disney conglomerate—on ABC's most successful contemporary, Black-cast comedy. On the one hand, it follows in a long line of media conglomerates using the companies they own to promote their other brands. *Blackish*'s 2016 episode "VIP" and *Modern Family*'s (ABC, 2009–2020) 2012 episode "Disneyland" both function as commercials for the network's sister enterprise Disneyland. On the other hand, as a series that I would argue was centrally concerned with what Blackness means/meant in a post-Obama and allegedly post-racial America, *Blackish* centers the importance of Blackness and Black representation through its *Black Panther* interstitial. In a voiceover, series star Anthony Anderson says:

> Superheroes: they save the day and beat up the bad guys and keep the cape industry booming. And the majority of them [sound of tape rewinding] don't look like me. Which is why when Marvel Comics finally introduced a Black superhero in 1966, it was a big deal. Black Panther, a.k.a. T'Challa uses his superior strength and intellect to fight evil and protect his people. T'Challa is the king of Wakanda—the most technologically advanced nation in the Marvel universe. [. . .] But what I find coolest about the Black Panther is the message he sends my kids. Because when you see a hero who looks like you, it helps you find the hero inside you.

It is unclear whether Anderson is speaking as himself or as his *Blackish* character Dre in the interstitial, but one thing is clear: either Anderson (who has two children) or Dre (who has four children within *Blackish*'s diegetic universe) situate *Black Panther* as a useful media text for Black children to see because of the presumed benefits of seeing "positive" Black role models in media. Media is thus imagined as a "looking glass" in which importance is placed on Black children seeing so-called positive images of themselves refracted back as they develop a sense of themselves.[36] Placing similar importance on *Black Panther* for Black children, Frederick Joseph, a New York–based author and marketer, created the #BlackPantherChallenge GoFundMe campaign, which "allowed more than 75,000 children worldwide to see *Black Panther* for free."[37] In short, in many segments of the American Black population, *Black Panther* was understood as particularly important for Black children to see, and Black *Black Panther* fans were no exception.

Black fans like Anson, 48, upstate New York, consumed *Black Panther* because of what he imagined it meant for future generations of Black people. He says, "I don't think that the film itself is just going to miraculously change everything for us. But I hope that it is the beginning of a trend in art that changes the way we think about ourselves and

Figure 2.4. Screengrab from the promotional interstitial video *Blackish* used to promote *Black Panther*.

discuss ourselves both in film and in broader media. And then for me what's really, really important is how my children, how they think about Black people, how they think about themselves." Anson raises a question about the limits of media like *Black Panther* to effect seismic shifts in Western culture's anti-Blackness. At the same time, he hopes *Black Panther* is the beginning of a trend in which Black filmmakers shift how they mediate Blackness across media forms. His use of his own clout, then, is partly to shore up support through *Black Panther* for a shift in how Black folks think of themselves within media culture, particularly for Black children. This use of clout is similar to the ways Black Misty Copeland fans used class to elevate her, as discussed in chapter 1. Like Anson, Arienne, 32, College Park, Pennsylvania, used her clout to attempt to make *Black Panther* successful partly because of her nephew. She says her nephew "loves superheroes. And recently, he has started talking about *Black Panther*. I'm just really excited because . . . I mean, he's a kid. He pretends to be superheroes all the time, but this is going to be the first time that there's a superhero who actually looks like him." Nikki, 52, of Atlanta, adds, "And not everybody has to be like, you know, royalty like the T'Challa and his family. They can be like a Nakia, who is a really tough warrior. But [Black children] can be these awesome people and *Black Panther* gives them something to look up to: [characters who are] multidimensional [and have] various layers. You know what I mean?" Similarly, Clarence, 30, Detroit, argues that "kids seeing themselves represented as superheroes is awesome. When you're a kid, you look up to superheroes more than you look up to real life people." Lastly, Kristal, 37, Tampa, hopes that *Black Panther* inspires "kids to make [Wakanda] real. Let's get out there. Let's get educated. Let's teach our kids to, like, value education [. . .]. So, [*Black Panther* and Wakanda are] about hopes and dreams and I hope that's what people take away from it." For Black fans like Anson, Arienne, Nikki, Clarence, and Kristal, Black clout is centrally concerned with Black futurity. If, as cultural theorist Kodwo Eshun argues, Afrofuturism is partly preoccupied with "correcting the history of the future," then these Black fans understand *Black Panther* and Wakanda as key to an Afrofuturist world for Black children.[38] Collectively, Anson, Arienne, Nikki, Clarence, and Kristal understand media as a looking glass for children, who they imagine are susceptible to mediated images. As such, this use of *Black Panther* by its Black fans underscores how *particular* mediated images activate Black folks' consumption practices by doing it for the future of the culture. Clout, in this instance, is an investment in the present to ensure a different Black future.

Stephanie, 48, Ypsilanti, Michigan, adds that the film was particularly important for her daughters. She said:

> My oldest [daughter], who did go see the movie, she was like, "This is awesome. The women were awesome." I want to encourage that kind of bad assedness [. . .]. With *Black Panther*, I think it would be easy to focus on this masked man in a suit, and not necessarily all the other people who were a part of it. I think the women are equally important to me and to my . . . the fact that I have girls [. . .] it is important 'cause I can be like, "You see? They are out here doing this. They are out here whooping ass and taking names. That's what's happening." I feel that representation is important, so I'll do what I can to support that.

Stephanie understood *Black Panther* as a feminist film for her daughters because it mediated Black women as strong warriors and not damsels in distress or women who use their sexuality as power. Similarly, Kina, 42, St. Petersburg, Florida, adds that films like *Black Panther* are important because they give children, particularly girls, the opportunity "to look at the screen and say, 'Oh, Shuri makes being smart and being into tech . . . She makes it look cool. I can do that. I can look at that, and I can do that.'" Stephanie and Kina center the importance of *Black Panther*'s focus on Black women, their strength, their intelligence, and their desirability as attributes that make the film important with respect to the intersection of clout and an image's imagined suitability for Black girls. As a reception practice, in certain ways, Stephanie and Kina retool *Black Panther* to center the women of Wakanda because of the Black girls in their lives. And in doing so, they similarly see the women of Wakanda as helping the Black girls in their lives imagine futures that might focus on science, technology, engineering, and math (STEM). Actress Geena Davis, founder and director of the Geena Davis Institute on Gender in Media, suggests that the mediated absence of women and girls in STEM careers "has a real impact on young viewers' ideas about themselves and the occupations they pursue."[39] Davis's introductory remarks on the institute's website suggest that "the factors that contribute to women's slim presence in [STEM] are undoubtedly complex, but we know that media play a contributing role."[40] Echoing the concerns Stephanie and Kina raise, the institute's report centers the ways representation presumably matters for how girls can imagine their futures. It is that investment in Black children's futures that moves Black folks like Stephanie and Kina to expend their clout on films like *Black Panther*.

Presumably, adult's assessments of the importance of *Black Panther* for Black children were correct, demonstrating that their decision to flex their clout by financially participating in its commercial success was not for naught. Upon *Black Panther* star Chadwick Boseman's 2020 death from colon cancer, many parents took to social media to demonstrate how the "Black Panther's" death affected their children. On a now deleted Facebook post, a user detailed her son's affective response to Boseman's passing. She wrote, in part, "my brown skinned baby had a super hero [sic] who looks like him. . . . and his heart broke yesterday." While

Figure 2.5. Stephanie and her family pose for a photo before seeing *Black Panther: Wakanda Forever*. Photo provided to author by Stephanie. Used with permission.

certainly in the social media marketplace in which the primary currency is "likes" and "shares," space should be held for parents either exaggerating and/or staging photos of their children to accompany sentiments around the importance of *Black Panther* for Black children, the fact remains that at the very least there is something affectively effective about what *Black Panther* meant, and continues to mean, for Black children.

Thus, the import Black *Black Panther* fans put on consuming the film in its initial theatrical release partly revealed itself in children's responses to the passing of its titular character. These responses demonstrate "the ways actors, the characters they play, and their celebrity status become inextricably linked within cultural production" and audience reception.[41] Children's responses, as remediated through their parents in social media spaces, make no distinction between Chadwick Boseman and T'Challa/Black Panther. This partly validates the clout Black *Black Panther* fans flexed en route to helping the film achieve its blockbuster aspirations. It also demonstrates how Black clout as a Black fannish response is linked to ideals about the future of Blackness in mediated spaces and the imagined importance of "positive" media images for Black children and their Black futures.

Rooting for Everybody Black

Clout, as a Black fandom practice helps to demonstrate how consumption, pleasure, and the long history of Black activism coalesce. The very real connection between money and power is one of the ways Black fans (and Black consumers generally) register their love for particular media texts. If money talks, then by consuming *Black Panther*, Black fans spoke loudly and clearly with their dollars—they made up more than one-third of the film's opening weekend haul.

Black fans used their clout to make the film a financial success for Disney/Marvel hoping that would result in more productions like it. But that does not necessarily mean the mainstream media industries rushed to greenlight more big-budget Black-cast films. While it was already in production as *Black Panther* was hitting movie theaters, *Harriet* was made for a modest $17 million. Spike Lee was given between $35 and $45 million to make his 24th feature-length film, *Da 5 Bloods* (2020). And both *King Richard* (2021, dir. Reinaldo Marcus Green) and *The Woman King* had $50 million budgets. To be sure, $50 million—or even $17 million—is a far cry from the $500,000 studios typically doled out to produce Blaxploitation films (adjusted for inflation, in 2023 a film like *Shaft* would have been budgeted at $3.36 million). But the Black-cast films released post-2018 never quite reached the budget

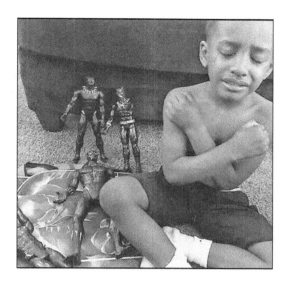

Figure 2.6. Images from various social media posts of children mourning the death of Chadwick Boseman/T'Challa. Images provided by posters. Used with permission.

heights of *Black Panther*. Certainly, 2022 saw the release of *Wakanda Forever*, which "bested" *Black Panther*'s budget by $50 million (or one *The Woman King*). Where Black-cast films like *The Woman King, Da 5 Bloods*, and *King Richard* were understood as Black films (and budgeted "accordingly"), the "Marvelness" of both *Black Panther* and *Wakanda Forever* signaled the ways media industries, despite Black folks flexing their clout and consuming media industries output in traditional ways (rather than seeing it through informal distribution networks like bootleg copies of the film), treat Black clout as useful for the bottom line, but not necessarily useful in making budgeting and greenlighting decisions.

On the one hand, Black fandom practices are not dissociated from the realities of an inherently racist industry that configures Blackness as a monolithic market from whom capital can be extracted. On the other hand, the pleasure Black fans find in feeling seen and, quite frankly, enjoying an afternoon or evening at the multiplex cannot be discounted. Black *Black Panther* fans certainly saw the film to demonstrate their commercial viability, but Black joy was ever-present in the ways Black folks went to *Black Panther* dressed in their best and marveled at the images and storytelling that unfolded before them. And while *Black Panther* was certainly a partly ephemeral theatrical event, it could be enjoyed again through syndication, streaming, and home video—particularly because of the importance many Black fans placed on the film as a source of role models for the children in their lives. Put simply, Black *Black Panther* fandom is as complex as it was a moment in Black cinematic history. It required negotiation between understanding the fickle whims of Hollywood production, the desire to see Blackness and have Blackness be seen, and the power of the Black dollar. In its negotiation of the politics of the media industries, Black *Black Panther* fandom was invested in and hoped for a Black future for the next generations of Black folks that might look something like Wakanda.

At the same time, the first C of Black fandom, *class*, is not absent from the discussion of *clout*. Black fans distinguish *Black Panther* from other films on which they could use their clout. And like Misty Copeland's Black fans, Black *Black Panther* fans hold the film and the characters within it up as suitable role models for Black children. And importantly, both Misty Copeland's and *Black Panther*'s Black fans use their Black look to effect change from the ballet theater to the movie theater.

Together, the first two C's of Black fandom have most closely illuminated the pains associated with Black fans in the joy/pain dyad I set forth in the introduction. The Black look has been utilized to attempt to affect representational and industrial changes. The next chapter begins the shift to the joys of Black fandom by examining Black *canon* formation as a Black fandom practice.

3

Canon

The Wiz, *Interpretive Communities, and Black Fandom*

I begin this chapter with meditations that helped conceptualize it. The first thing that occurred was my belated viewing of the music video for Alicia Keys's song "Teenage Love Affair." In it, Keys uses imagery from the Black canonical film *School Daze* (1988, dir. Spike Lee). The video demonstrates the ways some Black-cast texts are passed down between Black generations. Keys was only seven years old when the film was released, and as such, I suggest that either someone older than her passed down the knowledge of the film to her, or she engaged with people who understood the film's importance to Black culture. Particularly speaking to the intergenerational pedagogy of *School Daze* and Keys's music video, one of *School Daze*'s principal actors, Giancarlo Esposito, appears in the video to explicitly tie it to the original film. This intergenerational passing of particular Black texts is part of what I call *Black intertextuality*. Black intertextuality does not necessarily depart from the ways literary and media scholars (among others) have theorized intertextuality as the interplay between texts; where Black intertextuality differs is that it relies on a specifically Black canon for its intertextual referents.

Second, I saw a joke on Twitter that went, "Five members were in a group called The Temptations, all of whom were named Paul, Eddie, Blue, Otis and David Ruffin. Two went to see about David. Three saw Eddie leave off the stage. One went to Blue's funeral. More than five saw Paul drunk. How many came to see Otis?" The answer is "nobody," as extracted from the line of dialogue "Ain't nobody coming to see you, Otis" from the television miniseries *The Temptations* (NBC, 1998). This joke, and how Black folks know the answer, suggests that certain texts within Black popular culture become central to Black cultural literacies. That is, Black folks have been educated in a particular cultural knowledge base that centers the legacies of Black popular culture. Black

Figure 3.1. Stills from Alicia Keys's music video for "Teenage Love Affair" (top) that refashions imagery from Spike Lee's *School Daze* (bottom), demonstrating the intergenerational pedagogy of Black fandom.

Figure 3.1. (*Continued*)

cultural literacy is also observable in the previous example from Alicia Keys's "Teenage Love Affair" music video.

Third, I was absent-mindedly listening to hip hop group Little Brother's 2005 record *Chitlin' Circuit* while working. I had never listened to the record before, and much of it remained background music on my first listen. However, track 13, "Flash and Flare," shook me from work mode. As its central hook, "Flash and Flare" uses a part of "Red" from *The Wiz*'s (1978, dir. Sidney Lumet) Emerald City sequence, in which

Bella Devereaux is with **Shameka Green** and **2 others**.
Apr 13 at 9:42 PM · 🌐

Since y'all so SMART‼️ 5 members were in a group called, The Temptations all of whom were named Paul, Eddie, Blue, Otis & David Ruffin. 2 went to see about David. 3 saw Eddie leave off stage. 1 went to Blue's funeral. 5+ saw Paul drunk.

How many came to see Otis?

 567   602 Comments · 6.6K Shares

Figure 3.2. Facebook post uses a word problem about the made-for-TV film *The Temptations* to demonstrate Black canonical knowledges.

the Emerald City citizens inform listeners and viewers that one has "to have flash and flare" to wear the color red. The use of the song from *The Wiz* demonstrates not only how Black intertextuality and Black cultural literacies work within Black audience reception, but the ways Black artists retextualize iconic songs, films, and television programs by Black artists. In the retextualization, they do not necessarily attempt to give the new text a new meaning. Little Brother's retextualization of "Red" remains a comment on Black style. And "Flash and Flare" is concerned with expanding the ways *The Wiz* can be understood as an important Black referent for discussing Black style.

Fourth, in my last semester of PhD coursework, I read something that shook me to my core. Film scholar Christopher Sieving wrote that *The Wiz* was one of the "most spectacular flop[s] in Black-themed film history.[1] It is not that I disbelieved Sieving; it was simply that this was news to me. *The Wiz* was nothing short of a success in my mind—artistically and financially. Artistic triumph is certainly subjective, and my love for Diana Ross may have colored the ways I read artistic success onto the film. Yet, with respect to the film's financial success, *The Wiz* had always been important and available to me. It aired annually in syndication in Detroit, and it also ran at the Norwest Theatre, a second-run Detroit movie house, to enthusiastic Black audiences when I was a kid. So I simply assumed its success. I asked a group of friends with whom I have been close since our freshman year at Detroit's Renaissance High School, and with whom I share *The Wiz* fandom, the same question. This group, colloquially known as the Potluck Crew (Potluck), is comprised of Erica, Cory, Ayanna, Rhea, Roy, and me. They were similarly surprised when they discovered *The Wiz* did not recoup its budget in its original theatrical run. Ayanna, 48, says, "I was surprised to learn [of *The Wiz*'s box office failure] as an adult." Rhea, 49, adds that *The Wiz*'s failure was surprising to her because she "loved it as a child and followed what I thought was a brilliantly real depiction of Black folk in Oz." This assumption of brilliance and success shaped and continues to shape our fannish engagement with the film. And Sieving's factually true statement illuminates how distinct taste cultures structure engagement with media. For me, Potluck, and many Black folks, the financial and industrial success of *The Wiz* never factored into our calculus of the film. The terrain on which we evaluated *The Wiz* had little to do with its importance for Universal, the producer and distributor of the film. We engaged *The Wiz* on a different terrain: Black feeling.

These four disparate examples help illuminate the central concern of this chapter: Black *canon*. When I use the term *Black film canon*, I do not mean some official list designated by critics or academics; nor do I mean to refer to the ways fan canon has been described "as the ideas and concepts [. . .] fan communities have collectively decided are part of an accepted storyline or character interpretation."[2] Rather, by invoking the notion of Black canon, I refer to a collection of Black-cast media, like *School Daze*, *The Temptations*, and *The Wiz*, that seem to speak the language of Blackness *to* Black fans. Canon is not untethered from the other three C's of Black fandom in *Fandom for Us, by Us*. Rather, canon is similarly informed by class, clout, and comfort. Black fans still choose Black canonical texts over other Black-cast texts, and they also find comfort in the repeated consumption and mastery of these Black canonical texts. In this chapter, I use *The Wiz* to elucidate how Black fans understand Black canonical texts and their importance to Blackness and Black culture.

Methodologically, this chapter proceeds in two co-constituting directions. First, I use TikTok to show how the key components of Black canon, as I am theorizing it here, exist outside of the small group of Black *Wiz* fans I interviewed. By searching TikTok using the keyword "The Wiz," I found a host of publicly available videos/posts/stitches. I use these videos to lay the groundwork for my theorization of Black canon. As an ethical practice, I use the TikTok users' handles because I want to credit these Black content creators for their assistance in helping theorize Black canon. Second, after explicating the broader circulation of *The Wiz*'s position as a Black canon object, I move to in-depth interviews with Potluck, a group of friends who are also Black *Wiz* fans to show how the theory works "in action." I use a three-hour Zoom chat the six members of Potluck had on January 15, 2021, to discuss our *Wiz* fandom. While I served as the interviewer/researcher, as a Potluck member, I was/am also a participant. Thus, I position myself as what sociologist Patricia Hill Collins calls an "outsider within"—I am simultaneously an insider because I am a Potluck member, but I am also separated from Potluck as a researcher.[3] Because I am an outsider within—a Black *Wiz* fan studying Black *Wiz* fandom, this chapter is also partly autoethnographic. That is, I use autoethnography to "describe and systematically analyze [. . .] personal experience" and engagement with *The Wiz* to understand its Black canonization broadly while investigating its long-standing Black fandom.[4]

Concomitantly, because I am arguing that canon and community are co-constituting, this chapter positions Potluck as an interpretive community. Building on women's studies scholar Jacqueline Bobo's theorization of Black interpretive communities, I center this Black group's ability to weave a sense of Blackness, Black culture, and Black film as genre into their fannish attachments and behaviors.[5] Additionally, race and technology scholar Sarah Florini's work on Black fandom enclaves is useful in my engagement with Potluck. She argues that "enclaves allow Black fans to engage in a culturally inflected fandom that uses Black culture to interpret and celebrate their beloved media text."[6] In other words, as literary scholar Stanley Fish suggests, interpretive communities use their shared experiences to "determine the shape of what is read."[7] Part of my

Figure 3.3. The Potluck Crew in 1996 and re-creating the image in 2019 while celebrating 30 years of friendship.

positioning of Potluck as an interpretive community is bound within my assertion that community has a constitutive relationship to canon. That is, Black canon builds community just as much as community builds Black canon. In the sections that follow, I move toward a theory of Black canon not only to theorize the term, but to distinguish Black folks' canonical reception practices from cultish ones.

Toward a Theory of Black Canon

In using *canon* as a term, I recognize the raced, classed, gendered, and sexualized ways it has been deployed to valorize "great white men" above others. However, I do not want to completely throw away the term because it has been used in certain circles to underscore racist, (hetero) sexist, and classed distinctions. I do want to center how the selection of films for "canonization" are part of specific taste cultures. Thus, I use canon to suggest that there is no singular canon, but there are *canons* that can shift across temporality and affinity groups. As such, I begin my exploration of canon with film and media studies scholar Janet Staiger's suggestion that canonized film are those "chosen to be reworked, alluded to, satirized, become privileged points of reference, [and/or] pulled out from the rest of cinema's predecessors."[8] In discussing the politics of film canon formation, Staiger suggests that filmmakers, scholars, and film critics (both "academic" and "lay" critics) are key players.

Continuing the "gatekeeping" function but shifting to *Black* film canonization, African American studies scholar Lisa Alexander suggests that building an "academic film list with films that would typically be restricted to the popular list" would "chart the increasing number of voices that tell black stories" in order to "examine [the] ways in which the representation of black characters and black communities have progressed and regressed over time."[9] At least two points are important in Alexander's discussions around Black canon. First, she continues to forward that the Black canon is an "academic list," configured by those with the power and cultural capital to gatekeep such a list. Second, and related, the Black film canon Alexander suggests is one that is tied to representation as the analytic framework for canonization. While representation is certainly tied to taste cultures, it is often dissociated from pleasure and, instead, such an analysis compares images to tropes (often construed as "negative") and evaluates these simulacra against their presumed effect on viewers.

Both Staiger and Alexander provide useful starting points for the work I undertake in this chapter. From Staiger, my theorization of Black canon is concerned with Black-cast films that are reworked, satirized, privileged, and separated from the vast catalogue of Black-cast films that could be included. From Alexander, I build on her suggestion that Black canons should include films that would more often be understood as "popular" among Black audiences and fans. Cultural theorist Stuart Hall, discussing the notion of popular culture, argues that it "always has its base in the experiences, the pleasures, the memories, the traditions of the people. It has connections with local hopes and local aspirations, local tragedies, and local scenarios that are the everyday practices and the everyday experiences of ordinary folks."[10] In centering the popular, then, my theorization of canon is most deeply rooted not in which films gatekeepers signify as great, but instead, it centers audience pleasure generally, and Black pleasure specifically. Or, as classics scholar Ahuvia Kahane suggests, I want to move "toward the notion of canon as a socially embedded practice."[11] In short, Black canon, as I am theorizing it, is a Black fan practice.

In theorizing Black canon, I center Black taste cultures and fan practices not as aberrant, but as normative and central. In other words, I rebuke the notion that Black folks have developed a counter canon. I recognize that "counter canon" definitionally signals, as film scholars Sarah Benyahia and Claire Mortimer suggest, "the limitations of the traditional canon."[12] But, I argue that the alleged "traditional" canon is always already limited because it privileges (white) academic tastes rather than (Black) popular/fan/audience tastes. However, I depart from Benyahia and Mortimer's work insofar as they view the development of the counter canon as a response to the realization of "the impossibility of eradicating [the canon] completely."[13] In understanding canon as a Black audience/fan practice, the "traditional" white canon becomes moot. Building on African American philosophy scholar Lewis Gordon's work on Black aesthetics, my theorization of Black canon rejects white taste cultures in the valuation of Black canonized objects because doing so:

> offers a conception of equality beyond formal declarations of being so. As most whites don't seek legitimation of their aesthetic life from blacks,

blacks ceasing to solicit such from whites (and other groups dominating blacks) would be an act of equality in terms of what is absent—that is, the quest for recognition. This breaking out of the dialectics of recognition—of epistemic and aesthetic dependency, so to speak—has political consequences. In rendering white supremacist valuing, legitimation, and recognition irrelevant, the focus shifts to what Blacks can do to build different relations to the society and the self.[14]

In other words, Black canon is not a canon running counter to a "traditional" canon, nor does it have designs on eradicating it. Rather, it centers Black pleasure and Black joy outside of a contradistinction. The inclusion of "great" films into a Black canon more explicitly centers that "great" is affective. Certainly, in the white canon, "great" is also affective and subjective, but Black canon recognizes that Black audiences' often shifting taste cultures are the key drivers of canon formation rather than pretending such inclusion is objective or the terrain of "learned" scholars and critics.

There are three key points that undergird Black canon. First, at base, I center racialized media reception, which "is rooted in the racial divarication of Blackness in America."[15] Racialized media reception recognizes and centers the recognition of distinct Black taste cultures. What appeals to and resonates with Black audiences can sometimes be different from what appeals to and resonates with other racialized groups. Second, Black canon formation is mostly rooted in a reading of canonized films within their "dominant" codes; Black folks are not necessarily reading these texts "against the grain" in order to find pleasure and reasons to canonize them.[16] Black fans do not redemptively read *The Wiz* in the ways some white fans engage with cult film. Concomitantly, the very act of canonization is bound within group legibility. Black canonical films must always already be part of a broader and almost monolithic notion of Black communal knowledges, but they do not depend on group viewing for the pleasures they provide. Lastly, Black canonical films, like *The Wiz*, are part of an intergenerational Black communal knowledge wherein Black parents center particular Black popular culture items and icons as important for their Black children and for Blackness more broadly. This is similar to the ways Black fans have taken up both Misty Copeland and *Black Panther*, as I detailed in chapters 1 and 2. Black canonization partly happens when the importance of certain Black texts like *The Wiz* are "passed down" between Black fan generations.

Together, these three points undergird how I am positioning canon in this chapter. My insistence on Black canon, rather than Black cult or cult generally, is rooted in the ways Black fans engage with texts. In the next section, I begin by underscoring why cult fails as a useful analytic for Black fans and their relationship to *The Wiz*. Then, I turn to Black TikTok creators who use *The Wiz* in ways that speak to its canonization within Blackness and Black popular culture.

White Cult/Black Canon

Throughout this chapter, I treat Black-cast film generally, and *The Wiz* specifically, as a genre through which canon can be examined. Thinking through *The Wiz* generically as a Black-cast film rather than a crossover film, or musical, or any other generic distinction, helps illuminate how Black fandom and canon are symbiotically linked. In writing about Black-cast film as genre, film historian Thomas Cripps suggests that such films "may be defined as those motion pictures made for theater distribution that [. . .] speak to black audiences [. . .] and that emerge from self-conscious intentions, whether artistic or political, to illuminate the Afro-American experience."[17] Cripps's suggestion that generically Black-cast films should "speak to Black audiences" structures how I am differentiating Black canon from white cult as a central component of Black fandom. *The Wiz*, despite its intention to be a crossover film through casting, production budget, and marketing, spoke (and continues to speak) a different language to Black viewers—one that makes the film almost illegible to white viewers, which, simultaneously, structures their own cult reception practices.

Film scholars Ernest Mathijs and Xavier Mendik forward that cult films typically have at least some of the following six qualities: (1) an "active and lively communal following"; (2) audiences "at odds with the prevailing cultural mores"; (3) transgressive relationships to "good and bad taste"; (4) "intertextual references"; (5) "troublesome production histories, colored by [. . .] failures; and (6) "continuous market value and a long-lasting public presence."[18] To demonstrate how *The Wiz* functions largely as a white cult text for white reviewers and spectators,

I turn to both its historical reception and its contemporary marketing. White reviewers like the *New York Post*'s Archer Winsten mark several of Mathijs and Mendik's understandings of cult. Winsten writes, "In short [. . . *The Wiz*] could fool the wiseacres, like *Grease* which raced to popularity under its tremendous head of publicity steam, but I suspect it won't happen here, except with specially interested audiences."[19] I argue that from its inception, white press positioned *The Wiz* as reflecting three of Mathijs and Mendik's components of cult: first, opining that *The Wiz* needed to "fool" audiences suggests that it is a film positioned as "at odds with [white] prevailing cultural mores." Second, in its alleged attempt to "fool" audiences, Winsten suggests that in being out of step with "good taste," *The Wiz* would appeal only to those with transgressive relationships to taste. Lastly, in suggesting that the film would likely fail, Winsten simultaneously centers failure and the notion that the film was created for "specially interested" (read: Black) audiences more than white ones.[20]

In white reviewers' insinuation that *The Wiz* was out of step with white tastes, the cultification of *The Wiz* continues contemporarily. For example, in marketing copy for its Music Mondays series, Alamo Drafthouse, a specialty movie theater chain, described *The Wiz* as telling the story of "Dorothy [who] is now a shy 24-year-old Harlem kindergarten teacher played by Diana Ross. If that doesn't instantly make you curious enough to catch this insanely original movie maybe the rest of the synopsis will," before concluding that it is "about as original and crazy as a musical version of THE WIZARD OF OZ can be."[21] Discursively, the marketing copy centers (bad) taste in its positioning of *The Wiz*. Like much of the industry lore around *The Wiz*, Diana Ross's casting (and the aging of Dorothy into adulthood) is understood as one of the key things that marks *The Wiz* as a "bad" object—but, like cult objects, *The Wiz* is understood as so bad it is actually "good," positioning its (white) spectators/fans as preferring "strange" or "crazy" content that "transgress[es] common notions of good and bad taste."[22] But the Black generic landscape of *The Wiz* was, and remains, different.

Looking at *The Wiz*'s reception in Black press, Black reviewers decoded the film's industrial importance in two key ways: they "seized on the notion that *The Wiz* was decidedly not a Blaxploitation film," and secondly, they "often underscored that the future of Black-cast films in

Figure 3.4. *The Wiz* promotional copy on the Alamo Drafthouse website.

Hollywood hinged on the success of *The Wiz*."[23] *The Wiz* was discursively imbued with the power and possibility to change Hollywood's approach to celluloid Blackness, or what *Amsterdam News*' Marie Moore hoped would be "the beginning of a new era of lucrative and qualitative Black films."[24] Put simply, Black press, and I argue, Black viewers by extension, imported some of the strategies and tactics learned during the Black Civil Rights Movement (like the Montgomery bus boycotts) to suture the politics of consumption to the politics of activism. Like the discourses I discussed in chapters 1 and 2 around Misty Copeland and *Black Panther*, Black reviewers and Black viewers, by extension, used *The Wiz* and their money to attempt to effect representational and industrial change.

And indeed, Black moviegoers in Detroit, where Potluck members were born and raised, flocked to see *The Wiz*. In the sole theater where *The Wiz* was shown in a predominantly Black area of Detroit, the film performed strongly, collecting $49,593 in its first three days.[25] In other words, part of my argument for *The Wiz* as a Black-cast canonical film is that it did not fail because Black folks chose not to see it. The fervor with which Black moviegoers saw the film suggests that Black people did not understand *The Wiz* as a "bad" film in its initial theatrical release. In its positioning by Black press, it was always an "important" Black-cast film. And through the generational passing of *The Wiz* from Black baby boomers parents to their Black Gen X children, the reverence to and importance of *The Wiz* to Black culture as a canonical Black text was similarly passed down.

Black canon formation, as I am theorizing it, is a Black communal reception practice that rests on at least four criteria: (1) an ambivalent relationship to the formal aspects of the film; (2) Black feeling as a reception response; (3) intergenerational cultural pedagogy; and (4) retextualization within everyday life. These four criteria frame how I theorize the intersection of Black canonization and Black fan practices in this chapter.

In the first instance, Black fans have an ambivalent relationship to the "look" of a Black canonized film in terms of its cinematography, editing, and other aspects of film formalism. That is not to suggest that these elements are not noticed or commented upon, but they are not the primary prism through which Black canonical films are evaluated. This ambivalence, allows, as philosopher Paul C. Taylor theorizes about aesthetic theory, for asking "deeper questions about the status or meaning of the concepts employed in aesthetic inquiry."[26] In eschewing a focus on aesthetic valuations, Black fans can dwell in the pleasures they derive from the text. And in so devising a Black canon, formalism recedes from the ways a Black canonical film is evaluated. For example, Black TikTok user @yoglenduh begins a video by saying she:

> stumbled across an egregious opinion. Now everyone who knows me knows that *The Wiz* is my favorite movie. But someone in 2002 said that *The Wiz* was a visually boring movie and I have never been more incensed. Now, having your favorite movie be critically panned is one thing but the fact that people don't understand this film is just mind-boggling. [. . . This person also said] the reason for *The Wiz* being "visually boring" is because Oz is supposed to be all sparkly and shiny, and [*The Wiz*] made it drab and boring. That was the whole point of the movie. Because why do you think the "Brand New Day" scene had all of the drab washed away? Did you even watch the film?

On the one hand, @yoglenduh acknowledges that the film may be construed as "drab and boring." On the other hand, the film's "drab and boring" look is set aside aesthetically because it makes sense narratively. And in its sense-making, it provides pleasure. Thus, as a Black canonized object, Black fans consume *The Wiz* as a whole text rather than one they poach and remix to derive pleasure from it.[27]

Similarly, aesthetics are eschewed in lieu of overall affective evaluations of the film. Black TikTok user @theenerdybunny posted a video of the big number by Evillene (the Wicked Witch of the West), "No Bad News," with a text overlay that reads: "Evillene was literally my favorite . . . she was an ICON <3," and used, among other hashtags, #legend #icon #classic. This user does not reveal *why* Evillene is her favorite, only that she is a "legend" and an "icon," in a "classic" Black-cast film. It is also important to note that @thenerdybunny specifically configures *The Wiz* as a "classic" film, not one that is a cult classic, which signals its resonance for Black viewers and, more importantly, its position within a Black canon.

Films understood as Black canon feature experiences and language that resonate as uniquely and specifically Black. In this way, the aesthetics of Black canonical films are not as important as the second component of Black fandom: Black feeling. I turn to the first song (after the "Overture") in *The Wiz* to begin this exploration. The song, "The Feelings that We Have," features a bridge that suggests that Black feeling is partly about the assurances provided by notions of Black community. As Aunt Em and her family sit around the Thanksgiving dinner table, she sings, "And I'd like to know it's there. The feelings that we have. When you know that you can come running to me whenever times are bad."[28] In other words, the song centers safe *feelings* within a Black community. The song's chorus further centers those Black feelings and the necessity of Black community in demanding, "Don't lose the feeling that we have."[29] Thus, the notion of feeling generally, and Black feeling specifically, is, I argue, central to a discussion of *The Wiz* and its fannish Black canonization.

Black feeling builds on film and media scholar Racquel Gates's suggestion that certain Black-cast media (in her case, "trashy" reality programming) provide Black audiences pleasure. These pleasures are derived, Gates argues, "from the collective [Black] experience of being systematically denied access to the aspects of the American Dream and/or neoliberal notions of success that most mainstream media offer."[30] As such, Black pleasure is partly found in being seen within media in ways that resonate with Black experiences. Black feeling also builds on Black studies scholar Tyrone S. Palmer's argument that Black feelings are broadly illegible to out-groups, principally because out-groups (especially white ones) deliberately (mis)understand Black feeling as aberrant.[31] Lastly, rhetorician Lisa Corrigan forwards that Black feeling is "concerned with Black existence and the possible production of Black selves in anti-Black nation-states."[32] I use Gates, Palmer, and Corrigan for my own theorization of Black feeling to think through the production of Blackness in anti-Black media industries and to examine Black pleasure within particular Black visual representation like *The Wiz*. Black feeling is closely related to resonance (which I discuss more deeply in chapter 4 with respect to *The Golden Girls*) in the sense that Black feeling cannot be calculated. Not all Black images or Black-cast media invoke Black feeling. It has little to do with whether Black audiences were hailed to the text or not. Rather, Black feeling is, as feminist scholar Susanna Paasonen argues about resonance, "often discovered by accident as certain images among hundreds and thousands stick, attract attention, fascinate, and encourage future revisiting."[33] Black feeling, then, is concerned with the ways Black audiences *feel* a text's Blackness and with the collectivity of Blackness as an organizing logic for how we feel media.

Black feeling does not necessarily refer to the narrative content of a film. Rather, it engages the overall affect of the film-viewing experience. Black TikTok user @theweekendwatch, upon discovering that Netflix had added *The Wiz* to its library, says, "I'm about to go watch [*The Wiz*] right now for . . . [sic] one hundred millionth time of watching it [. . .] y'all don't understand. This is like one of my favorite movies and I'm not even a big movie musical type of person but it's [sic] certain movies that, I don't even view them as musicals, because as I'm watching the movie and I know all the songs, it just kind of flows." Eschewing an aesthetic valuation of the film, @theweekendwatch speaks to a notion of "flow" that structures how she engages viewing the film. I argue that @theweekendwatch's invocation of flow speaks to two of Urban Dictionary's definitions of the term: watching *The Wiz* makes her feel "calm, cool, chill" while simultaneously invoking "a state of mind where one does not worry about time, money, material possessions [sic], but instead decides to relax and take life as it comes."[34] In short, *The Wiz* speaks to her Black feelings. Black TikTok user @sweetz_97 suggests that it is simply common Black knowledge that *The Wiz* is a superior film to *The Wizard of Oz*. She says, "it ain't never been no correlation between the two. Ever. *The Wiz* is an experience . . . *The Oz* . . . is a movie." In relegating *The*

Wizard of Oz to simply a movie while elevating *The Wiz* to an experience, @Sweetz_97 demonstrates an evaluation of the film that does not rely on providing any evidence of *why* the film is an "experience," but simply that it is. Because of the Black feeling it invokes.

Black feeling is narrative in the collective Black fear some of *The Wiz*'s scenes invoke. In the "Subway Scene," Dorothy, Scarecrow, Tin Man, and Lion must go through a subway station to continue to follow the yellow brick road to Oz. In the scene, they encounter a street peddler who unleashes a host of horrors including trash cans that attempt to devour Scarecrow, electric wires deployed to electrocute Tin Man, and subway columns that try to crush Dorothy. Many of the film's Black fans cite this scene as traumatic, with Black TikTok user @yonnachambers saying, "I know I'm not the only one. This Subway Scene in *The Wiz* was the scariest thing. I cannot watch *The Wiz* now [. . .] because this [scene] is just trauma." It is worth noting that she hyperbolically claims to not be able to watch the film while using a clip from the film to demonstrate why she allegedly cannot watch it. @colekaine similarly says, "This [subway] scene right here in *The Wiz* used to terrify me as a kid. And I promise you, to this day, I'm 22 years old, and it still terrifies me." And while I use @colekaine's video to highlight Black feeling, it is worth noting that as a 22-year-old, she, too, must have had *The Wiz* "passed down" to her by Black elders. Lastly, Black TikTok user @KingKookBr33z3 features text over his video of the "Subway Scene" that simply says, "This shit is still scary!" In short, *The Wiz* invokes collective Black feeling, even when based in fear. Even as one of its most memorable scenes is evaluated as "still scary," these Black fans continue to engage with the film, and the "fear" is part of *The Wiz*'s Black canonization because the text is viewed as a whole rather than as a collection of discrete scenes or situations.

Third, Black canon films, like *The Wiz*, are important because our Black elders told us they were important. On the one hand, as sociologist Neta Yodovich argues, the intergenerational passing of fandom is about cementing "values and norms [. . .] through fandom socialization" while shaping and educating children.[35] On the other hand, intergenerational cultural pedagogy is Blackened through viewing a Black canonical text as "doing it for the culture" or what I have elsewhere called the exercise of Black "civic duty."[36] Part of what separates a "Black film" from the "Black canon" is the

Figure 3.5. Image from the "subway scene" from *The Wiz* that scared Rhea as a child.

way that failing to see, know, and/or understand a Black canon film like *The Wiz* can result in the revocation of one's fictional "Black card" whereas a lack of knowledge of, say, *Love Don't Cost a Thing* (2003, dir. Troy Beyer) will not. And like *The Wiz*, *Love Don't Cost a Thing* is based on white source material: the film *Can't Buy Me Love* (1987, dir. Steven Rash). But *Love Don't Cost a Thing* does not carry the same cultural weight as *The Wiz*. In short, I was sat down in front of *The Wiz*, but not *Love Don't Cost a Thing*.

Many TikTok users, alongside suggesting that the "Subway Scene" is terrifying, express that it was scary to them *as children*. User @Richonm posted a video with text revealing, "this was the most traumatizing part of this movie as a child." While I have already discussed the scene as part of Black feeling, I return to it here to center the last part of the text: "as a child." I argue that, for @Richonm to have seen the film as a child, her parents needed to allow her to watch it and perhaps even encouraged her to because it was important in some way. Similarly, @tita_la_cubana, who identifies herself as Afro-Cuban, suggests that "[e]very child of color needs to watch this movie" in her post about *The Wiz*. This intergenerational pedagogy structures the film's inclusion in a Black canon.

Finally, Black canon films work themselves into the vernacular of Black communities—or they are retextualized. Here I build on media studies scholar Taylor Cole Miller's work on retextuality. He defines the term as a kind of intertextuality that concerns the industrial practice of taking existing texts and giving them new meanings to fit television station brands via re-edits, new bumpers, and promos.[37] Miller defines retextuality in the context of television syndication and its invisible practices, but I adapt it to more explicitly discuss how fans retextualize, or broaden the meanings of, beloved objects, like *The Wiz*. Retextualization is a kind of intertextuality that explores how fans remix and "find" their beloved objects in other contexts. Importantly, intertextuality does not alienate those unfamiliar with the texts being remixed but functions as "Easter eggs" for those fans learned in the texts being remixed. Retextualization, then, is part of Black canon formation because of how it continues to position the relations between media objects. It demonstrates fan's mastery of a Black canonical text such that it can be mapped onto another text. But it is not "just" textual interminglings that are important. Rather, they help broaden textual meanings for fans. For example, according to some of her fans on TikTok, Beyoncé's Renaissance World Tour and its filmed version, *Renaissance: A Film by Beyoncé* (2023, dir. Beyoncé), retextualize *The Wiz*. After seeing TikTok user @Salondamarie's video in which she mentions connections between *The Wiz* and *Renaissance*, Reddit user Splinter's Apprentice lists the parallels she noticed. For brevity, I detail three of those retextualizations:

- **Dreams**: When Bey dropped *Renaissance* she said, "Creating this album allowed me a place to dream and to find escape during a scary time for the world." Dorothy adventures through the dreamland of Oz, on a pursuit to return home [. . .].
- **Live Feeds**: In Emerald City, there are little walking cameras that film the locals as they dance and pose, just like the cameras do throughout [the Renaissance World Tour . . .].
- **Home** (cont'd): At its core, *The Wiz* is the story of a journey, where in the end we're left to understand that what we seek out to gain, we've always possessed within. Sound familiar? [Lyrics from Beyoncé's song "Break My Soul":] "*We go round in circles round in circles searching for love. We go up and down, lost and found, searching for love.* **Looking for something that lives inside me.**" Scarecrow always had a brain, Tin Man always had a heart, Lion always had courage, and Dorothy, like us all, always had access to home." (emphases in original post)[38]

Like "good" intertextuality, Splinter's Apprentice's reading of Beyoncé's engagement with the film does not usurp whatever meanings Beyoncé encoded in *Renaissance*. Rather, *The Wiz* becomes a prism through which *Renaissance* takes on deeper meaning for Black fans. With respect to what Splinter's Apprentice terms "live feeds," the intertextuality is concerned with one-to-one correlations that can be observed; cameras roaming Emerald City in *The Wiz* mirror cameras roaming the audience during Beyoncé's concert film. In the case of "dreams" and "home," Splinter's Apprentice reconfigures *Renaissance* as a dreamland like Oz, and home "lives inside" as Glinda told Dorothy before revealing how she could return to her physical home. This retextuality also reveals how *The Wiz* is intergenerationally legible. If this fan's reading of Beyoncé's encoding is true, retextualizing *The Wiz* in *Renaissance* simultaneously reveals the intergenerational pedagogies of Black canon formation, as Beyoncé was not born until 1981, three years after the film was released.

This kind of retextualization can also be seen in other ways. For example, Black TikTok user @gigi1729 created a video wherein the Poppies, who are sex workers in *The Wiz*, dance while he sings a song using the melody from "Ease on Down the Road" but replaces the lyrics with "We done found the hoes." In other words, he does not change the meaning of the scene—they are still sex workers—but augments the initial meaning with contemporary language while using one of the film's most recognizable tunes such that the logic still makes sense. Lastly, TikTok user @ruthlesskween_ uses an extract from *The Wiz*'s "Brand New Day" scene with Dorothy and the Lion dancing. Within the film, the scene celebrates the liberation of Evillene's sweatshop workers, but @ruthlesskween_ uses it to embody, as the screen text for the video says, their "reaction to the [former president Donald] Trump indictment." Here again, *The Wiz* is retextualized to express Black feeling about a contemporary event without shifting its initial meanings.

These criteria are not necessarily discrete but are mutually constituting. Ambivalence about aesthetics is not dissociated from Black feeling, which is bound within an intergenerational cultural pedagogy. The ways elders pass on Black canon is imbricated in the ways Black canon fan objects are retextualized by Black fans. In the sections that follow, I use these four elements:—(1) ambivalent relationship to aesthetic valuation,

(2) Black feeling, (3) intergenerational cultural pedagogy, and (4) retextualization within everyday life—to further theorize Black canon as a central component of Black fandom practices using Potluck.

Ambivalent Relationship to Aesthetic Valuation

If aesthetics are a primary axis upon which the demarcation between white canon and white cult exists, *The Wiz*'s Black fandom demonstrates an ambivalence to those categorizations. As a beloved shared fan object, Potluck members are unsure if *The Wiz* is "good" from a formal perspective. Roy says, "I wouldn't classify it as a *good* movie because I feel like it's a remake. And I wouldn't classify it as a good movie in terms of story line because it's not an original story [. . .]. But I get a good feeling when I watch it because of the songs. I get a good feeling as I watch it because of the memories." For Roy, *The Wiz*, and his associated communal fandom, is wrapped up in his affective attachments. In other words, while he does not consider remakes "good" films because of their, in his estimation, lack of originality, *The Wiz* affectively overcomes those limitations. And the film can be elevated from considerations of its aesthetics through Roy's Black feelings. Rhea adds, "I define the movie as a good movie. Poor cinematography? Completely. Yet I'm struck by the length of time, with or without Potluck, that I would have probably still been connected to *The Wiz*. The connections and how it tells [. . .]and retells the story." Through a kind of negotiated reading of the film, Rhea, like Roy, suggests that watching *The Wiz* is about the feelings she has while watching it.[39] Ayanna says, "I mean, if a movie is bad, I'm not going to watch it anymore just like if the book is bad, I'm not gonna finish it. Like that's my definition [. . .]. Like some of [the technical aspects are] poor, but the storyline is there and it's still incredible and it still draws you in. And that's how I feel about *The Wiz* [. . .]. It must be a good movie because there's a bunch of horrible movies that I couldn't tell you even how they end. I can't give you two lines from them. So, it might not be good to other people, but it's good to me." Cory sums up the sentiment about the film by suggesting, "It's not a movie that I deem as a *great* movie, but [. . .] it's a great movie to me [. . .] I will always watch *The Wiz*." During our chat, I added that "there's something that is just so wonderful about ['Home'] and the fact that Diana Ross is believing this song so much that she literally starts crying. That is just so effective about the last moments of that film for me. The cinematography in that film is not innovative. Like the fact that 'Ease on Down the Road' with Diana Ross and Michael Jackson, is shot mostly in a wide shot from behind them. It's just like, 'What in the heck are you doing?' But there is still something about that movie that is just . . . Like even with all its shortcomings, I will ride for that movie." For the members of Potluck, the formal aspects of *The Wiz* are not what makes the film cohere as a fan object. Rather, the members of Potluck ultimately elevate Black feelings over "good" cinematography or original storytelling. Potluck members thus take an ambivalent stance around aesthetic valuations of the film because of their shared affect. While the members of Potluck were not in the initial imagined audience for *The Wiz* (we were two and three years old at the time of its initial release), our fandom gestures toward the ways certain Black-cast films "tap into a [Black] affective response, one that white reviewers and viewers perhaps" do not always understand.[40] As Ayanna and Rhea underscored, *The Wiz* and its lasting Potluck fandom is closely tethered to the film's watchability and the ways it has created connections—particularly among Potluck members. In eschewing aesthetics, Potluck does not rely on oppositional or alternative readings; rather they read the film "straight" as it enters into the Black-cast film canon and shapes their shared fandom.

Black Feeling

In the previous section, Roy discussed the positive feelings he had watching *The Wiz* even as he does not suggest that it is a "good" film. Rhea gestured toward the "connection" she (and, by extension, Potluck) has toward the film. And Cory ultimately detailed how the film might not be "great," but it is great *to him*. Taken together, Potluck centers how Black feeling is central to *The Wiz*'s Black canonization. In other words, for something to be taken up as a fan object, the *feelings* associated with it should be positive, or at the very least, productive (such that someone could oppositionally read the text or remix it).

Black feeling, as a component of canon, is partly contingent on Black cultural specificity. That is, not only should a text invoke Black feeling, but it should *feel* Black. For Potluck, *The Wiz* feels Black because of how it plays with and revises Black music and Black art. Erica states:

> I think what keeps me coming back is the music and the things that the music means to me. Interestingly enough, my favorite song as an adult have morphed into "The Feeling That We Have." It's like a mother's arms. It is just all of that where you feel nurtured and protected. So, when I hear that song, it's like I still feel, like, all right, someone's protecting me. What does [Aunt Em] say [in the song]? "When I lose my patience with you and I suddenly start to scream. It's only because I want you to be everything that I see in my dreams." Oh, I almost got a tear. [. . .] So, the music keeps you coming back and you recreate the place holders now. Like, when I'm having a pretty tough time at work, sometimes I think, "You can't win you can't break even. and you can't get out of a game" [from the Scarecrow's song "You Can't Win"]. And it's like, just deal with this shit. And it's, like, that's a fucked-up message.

The Wiz's soundtrack allows Erica to feel sonically visible within the film. As theorized by film and media studies scholar Kristen Warner, "sonic visibility operates as a tool that enables audiences the opportunity to not only feel represented by onscreen characters who look like them but also hear their culturally specific tastes, histories, and nostalgia through the soundscape."[41] In a way, then, *The Wiz*'s soundtrack hails Black audiences, like Erica, through what essentially remains Frank L. Baum's "white" story, but because of the music, feels Black. Ayanna continues discussing *The Wiz*'s sonic visibility when she says, "What drew me were just the Black folks and the music. I mean, *The Wiz* was all Black: everything in the music was all Black, everything. It wasn't Black folks singing white songs, it was like, 200 percent Black." For Ayanna, part of *The Wiz*'s import lies in how it depicts Blackness as its own creative force. In its creation of a Black sonic universe (created by the late composer Charlie Smalls with additional songs by the late Luther Vandross, and arranged for the film by Quincy Jones), *The Wiz*, with its Black A-list cast, activated Ayanna's Black feeling.

The Wizard of Oz does not invoke Black feeling for Potluck members. Cory says, "It's always about *The Wiz* for me [. . .]. I don't even know if I've seen *The Wizard of Oz* all the way through. I can't tell you that I've sat down and watched it in the past 40 years. You know, it's been on TV. But have I sat down and *watched* it? No." Similarly, Rhea adds, "I don't pause to think about *The Wizard of Oz*, unless I'm just trying to think about white people, heritage, thinking about the number of actors and actresses that came out of that. But I don't really attribute much to *The Wizard of Oz*. I could watch *The Wiz* over and over and over." For Cory and Rhea, *The Wizard of Oz* lacks the Black feeling they find in *The Wiz*. Black bodies on the screen do not always engender Black feeling. Rather, *The Wiz feels* Black to the members of Potluck because of *how* it mediates those Black bodies. As Rhea details, the first scene in *The Wiz* where Aunt Em and Uncle Henry are hosting the family for Thanksgiving dinner ignited Black feelings for her because it specifically takes the originary Baum tale and makes it Black—not just through casting, but through its action. Rhea says, "That whole dinner scene was . . . always one of the older cousins getting caught doing something [they shouldn't be doing] in somebody else's room. That whole scene was absolutely connected for me because you're like, 'Oh, this is what Black people do everywhere. This just ain't us,' [. . . and it] feels good." Underscoring these Black feelings, Roy adds, part of why *The Wizard of Oz* does not invoke Black feeling is because it does not "feel like a relatable piece of entertainment. A white girl from Kansas? It's just that it's not something that pulls on my heartstrings or brings me to a point where I go, 'Huh, that makes me want to go to Kansas now.' It makes me go, 'I'm not going to Kansas, they got fucking tornadoes and houses falling on people and ignorant white girls, I'm good.'" Despite how much of white-cast media content claims to be universal, for members of Potluck, *The Wizard of Oz* is a specifically white text that does not resonate like *The Wiz* does. Roy adds that it was *The Wiz*'s cavalcade of Black performers "who were at the top of their game around that time" that activates Black feeling in a way that *The Wizard of Oz* does not. Ultimately, its whiteness does not necessarily prevent Potluck members from appreciating, or even enjoying *The Wizard of Oz*. However, because *The Wizard of Oz* does not tap into Black feeling, it cannot become part of a Black canon, whereas *The Wiz* hinges on those Black feelings.

Intergenerational Cultural Pedagogy

Like the opening scenes of *The Wiz*, intergenerational Blackness is important for *The Wiz*'s Black canonization. Because all Potluck members experienced the film outside its original, first-run theatrical context, our exposure to the film was through our Black elders. Roy says, "Even people who were protesting [for Black Civil Rights] and all that weren't talking about [the stereotypes] in that movie. My mom was pro Black Panther as hell, she loves *The Wiz*. And made sure I did, too." Roy suggests that the film was still valued by elders despite the fact that it often traffics in what he considers stereotypical portrayals of Blackness; he specifically points to the costumes for Evillene's sweatshop workers and the ways the costumes exaggerate their posteriors: "in Evillene's factory, everybody had a big butt. That was part of the costume." He suggests that part of the pro-Blackness of the 1970s meant an embrace of *The Wiz* and all that was Black and beautiful in the period. Similarly, Cory recalls being introduced to the film by his Uncle Raymond and "watching *The Wiz* with him. Like we'd be, you know, just randomly sitting around and he'd be like [imitating Tin Man in the film] 'A teeny . . . a teeny' and we just burst out laughing. That's my memory of *The Wiz*. It was before I was 10 . . . for sure." As media and pop culture scholars Paul Booth and Peter Kelly argue, fandom can span "generations as more fans bring their families into the fannish fold."[42] At the same time, this intergenerational fandom is mostly rooted in ensuring that important Black culture is passed down generationally. It is a form of Black cultural education. While Roy's mother and Cory's uncle could certainly be understood as Black fans attempting to share their fan object with a younger generation of Black children, I argue that this intergenerational sharing simultaneously centers the importance of *canonized* Black cultural production like *The Wiz*. In other words, one of the artifacts of Black popular culture Black elders shared with Black children was *The Wiz*. Because my parents (particularly my mother) closely monitored the Black-cast media I consumed in an effort to "screen out" so-called "negative" representations, that *The Wiz* had my parents' "parental seal of approval" simultaneously gestures toward their representational politics and the importance they placed on *The Wiz* as Black canon.

Ayanna extends her 20th-century fandom of *The Wiz* to her children in the 21st century. She says, "I watched *The Wizard of Oz* with [my] kids, and like, they didn't have an affinity to see it again. But like *The Wiz*, the first time they saw it, they had to immediately see it again—and see it again and see it again and see it again." Given Ayanna's children's repeated consumption of *The Wiz*, it appears that a third generation of Black *Wiz* fans have been created, even as, much to Ayanna's chagrin, her daughter also affectively attached to *The Wiz Live!* (NBC, 2015). She says that they are "in a hot debate because she likes *The Wiz Live!*. I'ma keep her, and she's already been indoctrinated in the regular *Wiz*, but I don't know."[43] At least two points are worth exploring with respect to Black canon creation in Ayanna's comments. First, Ayanna uses the word "indoctrinate" to express how she exposed her children to *The Wiz*. She is attempting to teach her children to accept the 1978 film version of *The Wiz* as the superior text. At the same time, and not unrelated to the first point, Ayanna situates *The Wiz* as "regular" and everything else as derivative, and in some ways, inferior because it is not original. And more than that *The Wizard of Oz* is not the original. In the final analysis, Ayanna positions *The Wiz* as canonical for her children.

The intergenerational pedagogy of *The Wiz* is ultimately about its must-see Blackness. At the time of its release, Black press, in particular, centered Black people's "civic duty" to consume the film. It was at turns an important film for the representational cleavage it presented from so-called Blaxploitation films, and partly because its budget signified it as a "breakout text"; queer media studies scholar Andre Cavalcante theorizes "breakout texts" as texts that have three main characteristics: they break "into the cultural mainstream, [. . .] break with historical representational paradigms, and [. . . break] into the everyday lives of the audiences they purport to represent."[44] I adapt Cavalcante's work here to think through how the intergenerational pedagogy of canonized Black fandom functions. Because of *The Wiz*'s mainstream distribution (as opposed to the more niche distribution strategies of Blaxploitation films) and its gesture toward the Black fantastic, 1970s baby boomers took up *The Wiz* as a must-see text. *The Wiz* also broke into their lives, and they, in turn, ensured that it broke into the lives of their Gen X children. This pedagogy allowed *The Wiz* to become a Black canonical text that could connect generations of Black viewers and fans alike. That my mother introduced me to *The Wiz*, or that Cory's uncle introduced it to him, that Roy's pro–Black Panther Party mother reinforced the importance of *The Wiz*, or that Ayanna introduced the film to her children demonstrates the ways these intergenerational practices are concerned with developing, defining, and delineating *The Wiz* as Black canon.

Retextualization within Everyday Conversations

This section engages how Potluck uses *The Wiz* within and outside the group as among the ways the film is retextualized in the process of its Black canonization. I am interested in how Potluck uses the language of *The Wiz* as a site of insider knowledge *and* humor. This section builds on philosophy scholar Simon Critchley's suggestion that humor can be a "form of cultural insider-knowledge [. . . that] endows native speakers with a palpable sense of their cultural distinctiveness."[45] In other words, I am interested in how Potluck reframes, recycles, and reuses dialogue, song titles, and narrative events within *The Wiz* to generate a lexicon that is mostly comprehensible only within the group. Partly, I argue that Potluck functions as a subculture that uses intentional communication to open *The Wiz*, as sociologist Dick Hebdige explains, to new forms of textual readings.[46]

Erica says that *The Wiz*, its dialogue, and its music have become "just our lexicon. It's a part of our vocabulary just like when slang slides into the dictionary." She adds, "it is like a shared language. I know that you understand what I'm saying when I say, 'You can't win.' And then it's like it has a life of its own. It breathes." How Potluck deploys its lexicon functions mostly as a set of "in group" meanings that, while perhaps legible by "outsiders," take on different meanings within the logics of the interpretive community. For example, Roy says, "Al would say, 'Don't bring me no bad news [referring to Evillene's signature song].'" While the very sentiment of wanting only good news is, perhaps, universal, within Potluck, it references a song and a moment within *The Wiz* where it may just signal the sentiment to someone outside the group. At the same time, as I recalled, "The thing I remember that we share about *The Wiz* is saying, 'Yeah, Rhea's wearing rubies on her yacht.'" The line originates from the "Red" section of the Emerald City sequence, in which the fashionable Emerald City citizens discuss why red is in vogue. When deployed within the linguistic logics of Potluck, the line is used to demonstrate Rhea is behaving poshly—or wearing rubies on her yacht. In other words, many of these instances are legible outside the group, but because of the canonization of the film with the group, the line accrues extratextual meaning "as the text is appropriated and used by enduring fans."[47] At the same time, these retextualizations of *The Wiz* demonstrate how Black canon further sutured the Potluck community together through reuse of the film, and also how the Potluck community works to build Black canon.

Part of Potluck's retextualization of *The Wiz* can also be observed in the way the Tin Man's origin story moves from being one rooted in sorrow in the film to one that is decoded joyously in its canonization. The Tin Man is discovered on New York's Coney Island as Dorothy and Scarecrow trek down the yellow brick road as it moves through New York and its boroughs. The Tin Man was sat upon by his ex-wife Teeny as their relationship faltered amid the closing of the amusement park they had called home. This sorrowful origin story and Tin Man's crying whenever he mentions his ex-wife are recoded as joyful within Potluck. Like Black women's reception of Celie in the film adaptation of *The Color Purple* as discussed in feminist scholar Jacqueline Bobo's work, the sorrow is "forgotten" because Tin Man ultimately triumphs and finds the heart he thought he was missing.[48] But it also partly dovetails with what I have elsewhere called "rolling," or "the kind of uncontrolled Black laughter that results in tears or loss of breath. Rolling [...] is the way laughter is mixed with screams, shrieks, and Black signifying practices."[49] In rearticulating and recycling the Tin Man's "Teeny" cry, Potluck decodes his pain as something that, when extricated from the film, is resignified as joyous.

Retextualization within everyday life, as a Black fandom practice, centers how Black fans reuse and update references from beloved fan objects to maintain their vitality as Black canonized objects. The linguistic logics of Potluck's deployment and redeployment of lyrics and dialogue from *The Wiz* indicates Potluck's display of "mastery and proficiency" of the text within the group."[50] The mastery and proficiency, however, is not competitive. It is an exercise in which shared knowledge further sutures Potluck's strong ties and a process through which the film's canonization is demonstrated. In short, the community and its

Figure 3.6. *The Wiz*'s Tin Man (as portrayed by Nipsey Russell) crying over having been "felled" by his fourth ex-wife, Teeny. This sorrow is refashioned as humor through Potluck's canonization of the film.

logics are reconstituted through shared fandom of *The Wiz* as a Black-cast canonized film, while concomitantly, a Black canon is created by and through community.

Canon and Black Fandom

The ways Black fans canonize *The Wiz* are not fully divorced from the other C's of Black fandom. Black fans use class to distinguish between *The Wiz* and any other number of Black-cast films—and especially, with respect to this chapter, *The Wizard of Oz*—as they do with Misty Copeland. Black fans also used their clout to try to make *The Wiz* a financial success upon its initial theatrical release, as Black *Black Panther* fans did 40 years later. And Black fans continue to find comfort in reengaging with *The Wiz* as they do with *The Golden Girls*.

Black canon, as a component of Black fandom, is linked to *certain* Black texts. And while those Black canon texts can be visually "ugly," they are deemed "important" by trusted sources of intergenerational pedagogy. They are simultaneously ripe for the activation of Black feelings and the dialogue and music can be retextualized outside the text. This retextualization results in a fannish remaking of the text through language and visual style.

The act of Black canonization is inextricably linked to communal forms of Black fandom. The Black canon partly shapes the conferral (and revocation) of fictional "Black cards" for membership within the colloquial imagination of a universal Black community. At the same time, Black canonization is central to ideals about Black cultural production: there are some texts that are "for the culture" and speak to the culture. *The Wiz* is one such text. Canonization, when applied to Black media productions, demonstrates how Black fan practices work to shape Black cultural knowledges. The texts deemed Black canon are not necessarily those films, programs, and media figures that are "best" as much as they are those texts that are important as indicators of Black feeling, intergenerational cultural pedagogy, and retextualization.

Canonization, as a Black fandom practice, is communal because of the ways the logics of canon knowledge function. When the importance of particular Black cultural productions is passed from, for example, Roy's mother to him, or from Ayanna to her children, the text's legibility and longevity as a canonized fan object is solidified. As I've noted throughout this chapter, that the members of Potluck and many of the TikTokkers were not old enough to consume (or remember consuming) *The Wiz* speaks volumes about the ways our Black elders ensured exposure to the text—and how Ayanna passes that sense of importance on to her own children. The intergenerational pedagogy that is key to Black canon formation is connected to the Black feeling *The Wiz* invokes and evokes. The Black feeling is not necessarily about an aesthetic valuation of *The Wiz*: whether it looks expensive or cheap, or whether its continuity editing is effective. In fact, Black fans are ambivalent about how the film looks. Rather, the power of *The Wiz* is rooted in the feelings it recalls for Black viewers. Potluck, as Black fans of *The Wiz*, do not think about how *The Wiz* is Black as much as they focus on how it *feels* Black. And while parts of *The Wiz* like the Subway scene scared some Black fans, the overall Black feeling of the film is joyous. Ultimately, by eschewing aesthetics, learning about Black cultural productions from Black elders, and embracing Black feeling, Black fans retextualize *The Wiz* to make new and deeper meaning from a static fan object. But at the end of the yellow brick road, *The Wiz* is one of the beloved Black-cast films included in a Black canon.

4

Comfort

The Golden Girls, *Resonance,* and Black Fandom

Whenever the four "Golden Girls" who reside at 6151 Richmond Street in Miami gathered around the kitchen table to talk about life and love there was one constant: cheesecake. Cheesecake is a lot of things: it is delicious; it is dessert; and it is also comfort food. Cheesecake, like other comfort foods, is the kind of food often eaten in times of sadness and/or worry. It is also a type of food that can activate nostalgia and/or sentimental feelings. In this way, I argue "The Girls" used cheesecake to provide the comfort they needed to candidly discuss Dorothy's dating woes, Blanche's sexcapades, Rose's St. Olaf stories, and Sophia's invitations to picture Sicily. The series' narrative use of comfort food is fascinating because Black *Golden Girls* fans, more than 30 years after the series ended, use comfort to discuss their continuing fandom of the series. As a noun, *comfort* describes how feelings of grief or distress are alleviated and eased. But it also describes a state of physical ease and freedom from pain. Thus, in this chapter of *Fandom for Us, by Us,* I use comfort to frame Black *Golden Girls* fandom as a joyous deployment of Black fandom. Where chapters 1 and 2 highlighted the "work" of Black fandom, this chapter explores how Black *Golden Girls* fans do not *just* watch (and rewatch) *The Golden Girls,* but how they come to the text "with different agendas and desires" and leave it feeling comforted.[1]

Including a series about four old white ladies in a book about Black fan practices may seem odd. There is, however, a method to my madness: studying Black *Golden Girls* fans allows an examination of what I am calling a *politics of resonance*. In many ways, the other fan objects explored throughout *Fandom for Us, by Us* rely on a politics of visibility: the fan objects match the race of the fan. A Black politics of resonance concerns how Black fans are drawn to texts without Black stars or Black topics. Resonance concerns, as feminist scholar Susanna

Paasonen argues, "moments and experiences of being moved, touched, and affected by what is tuned to 'the right frequency.'"[2] For Black fans, the frequency to which *The Golden Girls* is tuned, as media studies scholar Kristen Warner argues about Black resonance, seemingly "understands that the experiences of the viewer are informed by a host of referents that at any point can be called out to hail them into the text."[3] Thus, a politics of resonance shifts representation from the terrain of "being seen," which gestures toward the visual, to the register of "feeling seen," which invokes an affective attachment to *The Golden Girls* even as Black bodies are infrequently depicted in the series. This politics of resonance is particularly important because, as Black *Golden Girls* fan Jay, 45, Decatur, Georgia, suggests, the advent of the streaming wars and the continued proliferation of channels and networks producing original content has resulted in viewers having myriad choices. He says, "Right now, we have choices before us. We have everything available. I would rather turn on *The Golden Girls* and watch that. Even though I know I've seen each episode at least four or five times each, I'll still watch those before I watch anything else." It is Jay's choice, and that of the other Black *Golden Girls* fans in this chapter, of the series among the sea of short-form media choices, both new and older content, that this chapter explores. But it is not simply the classed choice of *The Golden Girls* that is at the center of this chapter, but what Black fans get from the text also interests me. And as I argue throughout this chapter, Black *Golden Girls* fans, in engaging a politics of resonance around *The Golden Girls*, find that feeling seen when watching the text brings them comfort, like the cheesecake Dorothy, Rose, Blanche, and Sophia so regularly eat.

This chapter treats *The Golden Girls*' Black fandom as what media reception scholar Rebecca Williams theorizes as post-object fandom. She uses the term to describe series that "can no longer produce new texts," but whose fandom continues unabated.[4] Because of the deaths of its four leading ladies, Estelle Getty (2008), Bea Arthur (2009), Rue McClanahan (2010), and Betty White (2021), *The Golden Girls* cannot produce new texts. However, a tweet I sent on June 28, 2020, asking if there were any Black *Golden Girls* fans who would be willing to speak with me about their fandom ultimately netted 27 Black *Golden Girls* fans excited to talk about their love of the series. Through this process, I not only confirmed the strength of *The Golden Girls*' Black post-object fandom,

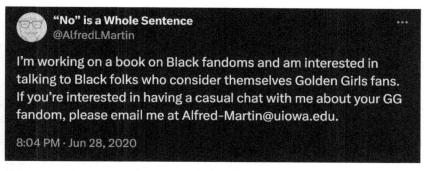

Figure 4.1. Twitter post used to recruit Black *Golden Girls* fans.

but I discovered that I was not the only Black *Golden Girls* fan in the world. We exist, but we are typically not included in the category "fan" of the show—until now.

Methodologically, this chapter uses 27 in-depth interviews with self-identified Black *Golden Girls* fans conducted between July and August 2020. These Black fans were recruited through Twitter (see sidebar for full descriptions of participants). While *The Golden Girls* stopped producing new episodes in 1992, the youngest of the Black fans with whom I spoke was 29 years old, having experienced the series (and their attendant fandom) entirely through syndication. The Black *Golden Girls* fans I interviewed range in age from 29 to 56 and live in major metropolitan areas like Philadelphia, Baltimore, Detroit, New York, and Washington, DC, mid-sized cities like Portland, Oregon; Louisville; and Oakland, and smaller towns like Waco, Texas; Stockton, California; and Superior, Colorado. The Black *Golden Girls* fans I interviewed identify across the sexual spectrum: gay, lesbian, pansexual, heterosexual, bisexual, queer, questioning, and fluid. The majority (20 of 27) of the interviewees identify as women and more than half (18 of 27) are single. These Black *Golden Girls* fans are overwhelmingly formally educated. One interviewee holds an associate's degree, while nine earned a bachelor's degree (three of whom were working toward a master's degree). Nine interviewees earned a master's degree (one interviewee is pursuing a PhD), and six respondents hold a PhD. The interviews were conducted via phone and lasted between 60 and 90 minutes.

I am the "invisible" 28th Black *Golden Girls* fan in this chapter. My own *Golden Girls* fandom began when I was a kid watching it on TV. Growing up in 1980s Detroit, Saturday nights, like most nights, were spent in front of the television (#LatchkeyKid). By the mid-1980s, my family had "graduated" from having one TV set in the household to three sets: one in our basement, which often served as the "family" TV; a color TV in my parent's bedroom; and a black-and-white set in the kitchen of our family home on Detroit's northwest side. As a preteen, I remember watching—and loving—*The Golden Girls*. I am certain many of their innuendo-laden jokes escaped my comprehension, but there was something that resonated with me when watching the four old white ladies who shared a home at 6151 Richmond Street. As a college student in the mid-1990s, after *The Golden Girls*—and even its spinoffs *Empty Nest* (NBC, 1988–1995) and *Golden Palace* (CBS, 1992)—had ceased production of new episodes, I religiously watched *Golden Girls* reruns on Lifetime before going to bed. As an adult, it has manifested in my running my first (virtual) 5K because it was called "Stay Golden" and included *Golden Girls* swag. Friends, family, and my godchildren often gift me *Golden Girls* games, T-shirts, and tchotchkes. My husband and I have traveled to San Francisco to see *The Golden Girls Live!*, a drag reenactment of episodes from the series. And I have traveled to New York and Chicago to visit the Golden Girls Kitchen as part of this research, but also as a fan of the series.

But what, precisely, is a Black *Golden Girls* fan? Because this book develops grounded theory, I use the definition given by Black *Golden Girls* fan Megan, 38, Atlanta, to guide this chapter and describe the people I interviewed. She says:

> To me, a viewer is someone who likes but won't go back to [*The Golden Girls* . . .]. I think as a fan, [the fan object is] something that you always go back to. You know? That you're always going to feel some type of way when you see each and every episode. It doesn't matter if you've seen it 100 times, when you see it, you still have those same feelings, you still understand it. And it can actually connect to different things that may be going on [. . .]. And you can connect with other people with it.

For Megan and the other Black *Golden Girls* fans in this chapter, feeling some type of way about *The Golden Girls* encapsulates, in the

Figure 4.2. Some of my *Golden Girls* fan merchandise including games, puzzles, and a cutting board, and an image of me moments after finishing the virtual "Stay Golden" 5k.

Figure 4.2. (*Continued*)

words of film and media scholar Racquel Gates, "the myriad feelings that do not fit neatly into socially recognizable categories. It allows for emotional messiness and complexity."[5] Feeling some type of way about *The Golden Girls* is about the sadness felt when watching Dorothy leave 6151 Richmond Street in the final episode, "One Flew Out of the Cuckoo's Nest"; the anxiety felt as Rose awaits the results of her HIV test in "72 Hours"; or the joy when Rose returns home after feeling she needed something else from life after a health scare in "Before and After." In short, as Blanche describes, "feeling some type of way" is like feeling "magenta." In the episode "Take Him, He's Mine," she describes magenta as "all kinds of feelings tumbling all over themselves. Well, you know, you're not quite blue because you're not really sad and although you're a little jealous, you wouldn't say you're green with envy and every now and then you realize you're kinda scared but you'd hardly call yourself yellow. [. . .] Magenta. No way to really explain it but, fortunately, between friends, you don't have to." It is feeling some type of way—or magenta—that I explore within this chapter. And even as the ultimate affective register Black *Golden Girls* fans feel for the series is comfort, it works through several emotions to arrive at that comfort. It is that magenta feeling and its reconciliation as comfort that animates the work in this chapter. These ways of making Black fans feel, I argue, are wrapped up in the act of providing, as film and media studies scholar Barbara Klinger puts it, "a guarantee of pleasure or satisfaction as well as a way to give a controllable shape to everyday existence."[6] These feelings are bound within the joy and comfort these Black fans find in the series.

Comfort TV and Black Fandom

Many people retreat to "trash" or "regular" television because these programs offer what film scholar Caetlin Benson Allot calls the "comfort of escape," where people use media as a salve.[7] Black *Golden Girls* fan Aaron, 49, New York City, echoes the series' function as escapist when he says, "The thing that would give me the most joy would be if they happen to be on TV and I would sit down, and I would just watch them. It was this pure sense of escape, more so than any other TV show out there." Aaron suggests that not all television is created equally. For him, there are only certain shows that provide him with the comfort of escape, and chief among those is *The Golden Girls*.

During the COVID-19 pandemic, rather than necessarily bingeing newer content, many viewers, like Aaron, turned to reruns, which, as media scholar Derek Kompare explains, are central to the television industry for the financial stability they provide in an unpredictable industry.[8] To Kompare's point, *The Golden Girls* has never been off television since the series stopped producing new episodes in 1992, bringing in steady revenue for its syndicator, Buena Vista Television, through reruns on channels and platforms as wide-ranging as Lifetime, Hallmark, Logo, and Hulu, among others. While Kompare approaches the rerun from a (mostly) industrial perspective, I want to shift to consider rerun viewing as an audience reception practice to underscore how the rerun provides audiences with affective stability. For example, a Hulu spokesperson told the *New York Times* that in April 2020, during the height of the COVID-19 lockdown, "Hulu viewers watched nearly 11 million hours of the vintage sitcom *The Golden Girls*."[9] I argue that the series' almost cyclical nature, which introduces new story elements, but none that inalterably change the series (except in the series finale, wherein Dorothy gets married), provides a comfortable rhythm for *The Golden Girls*' viewers and fans. That is, for *The Golden Girls*' Black fans, there is affective stability in the series' perpetual return to stasis. *The Golden Girls*, then, is comfort television because, as Vulture writer Kathryn VanArendonk describes the term, it is "repetitive [. . . and] disdain[s] hidden meanings and emphasize[s] clarity and immediacy over abstraction."[10] Similarly, TV studies scholar Charlotte Howell and art historian Joyce Howell suggest that comfort TV shows like *The Golden Girls* are not so-called "quality TV," yet they are not quite "regular TV."[11] For Black *Golden Girls* fans, the series brings them comfort partly because they know it so well that it cannot throw them narrative curveballs. As one example among many, Black *Golden Girls* fans know that while Rose is addicted to pain medication in the season 4 episode "High Anxiety," she will not die from an overdose. This familiarity, as Barbara Klinger argues, "enables viewers to experience both comfort and mastery. Foreknowledge of the story alters the narrative experience by lessening the tension associated with suspense [. . . .] Once viewers are conversant with a comedy's jokes [. . .]

they look forward to the laughs they know these jokes will bring."[12] And as many Black *Golden Girls* fans revealed, mastering *The Golden Girls* brought them laughs and comfort.

But not all older broadcast shows become comfort TV for Black viewers and fans. While Black folks were initially excited about series like *Moesha* (UPN, 1996–2001) being made available on streaming platforms, contemporary audiences engaging or reengaging with the series found some of its content, and even the series' titular character, troubling.[13] On the one hand, reception practices are temporally situated. A film, record, or television show might resonate in a particular moment, but when that moment has passed, so, too, has the resonance it provided. On the other hand, television programs like *The Golden Girls*, as the Black fans in this chapter demonstrate, retain resonance across time. For many Black viewers *Moesha* was decidedly not comfort TV, while *The Golden Girls* is received as such.

Comfort is often not *just* an affect but is comfort *from* something. Black *Golden Girls* fans like Ashlée, 38, Louisville, Kentucky, talk about the need for comfort during difficult times, like her mental health. She says she suffered a mental breakdown in her 20s and was "seeing a therapist and all that, but I always returned to *The Golden Girls* for the comfort I needed. I was just like, 'I don't have it together yet and life isn't looking how I thought it would look, but these girls are giving me a lot of comfort.'" She continues, "I think I knew I became a [hardcore] fan because I really do consider ['The Girls'] a big factor, along with therapy and meds, in helping me get through a really deep depression in my mid-20s. It sounds kind of naïve, but I don't think I could've gotten through everything that I went through without them, just because it was a consistent thing." The comfort Black *Golden Girls* fans like Ashlée find within the series during times of crisis suggests it provides consistency. As I previously discussed, the series will not throw fans narrative curveballs because they have already mastered the text. And in that consistency, fans develop a personal relationship with the series. Black fans create an affective bond with the characters, calling them "The Girls" as if they, too, are part of the Richmond Street crew. The series' consistency provides comfort for Black fans' engagement and reengagement.

THANK YOU FOR BEING A FAN: INTRODUCING BLACK GOLDEN GIRLS FANS

Aaron was born in 1974 and currently lives on New York City's Upper West Side. He is single, gay, and holds a master's degree. He works in Broadway advertising and makes more than $100,000 per year. Aaron's most vivid memory of watching The Golden Girls "must have been in the early '90s because it was at my parent's house and I was a teenager, and at this time The Golden Girls, if it wasn't still actually running, it would play weekday mornings on NBC[....] I just remember sitting there eating my breakfast, watching The Golden Girls and, the Frieda Claxton episode ["It's a Miserable Life," season 2, episode 4] comes on. And, of course, it was just normal because I did this any time that show was on, it would be on the TV. And I just remember when Rose gets very angry at Frieda Claxton and stands up and starts yelling at her. I remember being like, 'Oh my God, Rose is not as dumb as we think, she has guts, she has balls.' And she was just so fierce in that moment to my mind."

Alba considers herself a The Golden Girls fan because the "games and books and Funko heads that I have, make it go a little bit further than just a viewer. I have all four of them in Funko Pop and I have The Golden Girls Monopoly. And then I have a game that you play called Any Way You Slice It—a cute little game." Born in 1977 and currently living in Harlem, Alba says, "I am the person who watches The Golden Girls every night[....] I never thought about this until I spoke to you, but [...] to go to bed, I need something on. And so, I turn The Golden Girls on because I don't have to watch it to see it, because I know every episode. You show me the beginning and I'm like, 'Oh this is the episode where you get X, Y, and Z.'" Alba is a single, heterosexual woman who makes more than $100,000 per year. She holds a master's degree and works in human resources.

Ashleé was born in 1985 and identifies as bisexual. She works in journalism and "became aware of The Golden Girls in college because people in the dorms would watch The Golden Girls episodes, and Rue McClanahan even visited our campus and spoke, which I didn't go to because I wasn't a fan at the time." Ashleé currently lives in Louisville, Kentucky, and is a divorced woman who makes between $60,000 and $74,999 per annum. She says the proof of her Golden Girls fandom is her "cheesecake tattoo. It's just a slice of cheesecake. I drove from Louisville to Cincinnati to somebody who kind of specializes in the style of tattoos that I wanted and got it when I was like maybe 27 or so and I don't regret it all[....] For me, it symbolizes that I got through this really down time and that [*The Golden Girls*] helped me through. Like I said, I know this sounds sappy, but at the end of the day I can always just like sit down with some cheesecake and talk it out and it'll be okay[....] My tattoo reminds me of what I went through and what helped me. Really it was a lot of love and I got that from [*The Golden Girls*]. The way that those women loved one another and were there for one another, honestly now reflecting, I think taught me how to be a better friend because at the time when I was really, really depressed I didn't tell anybody. I was suffering alone because you got to be the strong Black woman, right?"

Brooke, a single, heterosexual woman who lives in Grand Rapids, Michigan, found out that I was looking for Black *Golden Girls* fans "on Twitter. I don't follow you, but in the feed, you know how it goes, other people like you or see it and I saw it. And then I think it was right around the time where Hulu said they're going to take off the blackface episode ["Mixed Blessing," season 3, episode 23]. And so, I love *The Golden Girls*. I have a board game, shirts, the whole thing." She was born in 1984, holds a bachelor's degree, and works in cybersecurity, where she annually earns between $60,000 and $74,999.

Charles is a pansexual man who currently lives in Philadelphia with his long-term partner. He was born in 1975, holds a bachelor's degree, and works in entertainment hospitality, where he earns between $10,000 and $24,999 annually. Charles describes himself as "Dorothy with a Sophia rising" because "I love Dorothy because she's the smart one and she's usually the voice of reason. Even when things aren't going the best in her own life, she usually gives good advice to everyone else and Sophia just because she's a smart ass."

Chinue's *Golden Girls* fandom is exemplified for her in the fan merchandise she owns. She says, "I have shoes, I have a number of T-shirts, I have Chia Pets, I have shot glasses, I have socks. I have calendars, yeah." She is a single lesbian, lives in Oakland, California, and is such a big fan of the series that much of the *Golden Girls* fan merchandise she owns comes from other people. She told me, "I had an ex-girlfriend who, I'm not actually sure where she found [*The Golden Girls* shoes] or if she had them made[....] They're sort of a high-top sneaker with the quintessential Miami leaf with all four Golden Girls printed on the sides of the shoes. They're really neat[....] I recently had a relative send me a [*Golden Girls*] T-shirt. Things like that where people think of me when they see *The Golden Girls*." Chinue was born in 1991 and holds a bachelor's degree. She works for a social justice nonprofit and earns between $60,000 and $74,999 per year.

Chris is a single, heterosexual woman who lives in Waco, Texas. She was born in 1988, holds a master's degree, and currently earns between $40,000 and $59,999 per year as a community college teacher. Chris has watched other friend-based sitcoms but differentiates her affective attachment to *The Golden Girls*. She says, "*Living Single* [Fox, 1993–1998] was like another one that I really liked kind of [because . . .] it's just like a community of women. Particularly like Black women on the East Coast and they were educated. So I really loved that one too, but I haven't gone back to it but [with *The Golden Girls*] having the DVDs and you know, it's on TV every day. So there's a level of accessibility that's been there."

Collett lives in Mt. Rainier, Maryland, and has "been watching *The Golden Girls* for really, as long as I can remember. I had a really strong older village growing up. So, I spent a lot of time with grandparents, a great grandmother, great aunts, and so on and so forth. And I still remember the sequence of *The Golden Girls*. I remember it was . . . *Amen* [NBC, 1986–1991] would come on. And then *The Golden Girls*[. . . .] I would sit and watch it with my grandparents or my dad, or you know, whomever. And it was just part of my childhood experience, and I've loved them forever." Collett is a heterosexual, single woman who was born in 1982. She holds a bachelor's degree and was working toward completing a master's degree at the time of our interview. She earns between $60,000 and $74,999 per year as a teacher.

Everyone in **Dorcia**'s life knows she is a *Golden Girls* fan. She says, "if they know me, they know that I love *The Golden Girls*. There's probably not a day that goes by that I don't recite a line because there are so many lines that are just so applicable in my life. My husband, he even got me, for my birthday last year, it's a drawing of *The Golden Girls* and someone drew me into the cast!" Dorcia is a heterosexual, married attorney who earns more than $100,000 per year. She lives in Fairfield County, Connecticut, was born in 1983, and earned a juris doctorate. She elevates herself from viewer to fan status because of "the length of time that I've watched it, I think right there, that [makes me] more than a viewer. You might consume something, but if you repeatedly and habitually and obsessively consume it . . . I think that's what elevates me to a fan."

Evan earned a bachelor's degree, works in event management, and earns between $60,000 and $74,999 per year. She was born in 1967 and currently lives in Austin. She says she discovered this study because "a very good friend of mine was on Twitter, and somehow she saw your tweet." Evan, a heterosexual, single female, says her friend "knows that I have plans for me and my group of girlfriends to... I want a *The Golden Girls*–style compound in our later years. So I am literally already saving to have a plot of land, build a house on it. I don't want to share a house, but you know what I mean. You have that sort of communal space. And I have talked about it for years. In fact, [my best friend] stayed at my house before and has been privy to the, 'Oh, I'm up in the morning? *The Golden Girls* comes on.' That's just what happens in this house. So, she's aware of it. She saw [the tweet], tagged me in it, and I was like, 'Okay. I'm in!'" Evan also considers Dorothy her role model. "I would consider, in many ways, Bea Arthur's character to be kind of a role model[....] I like her intelligence. I like her forthrightness. I appreciate, in a real way, those characteristics in her. And sometimes it bites her in the ass. I mean, she can be judgmental, as can I sometimes. But I identify with her."

Born in 1992, **Gabrielle** lives with her boyfriend in Pittsburgh. She holds a master's degree and at the time of our interview was a PhD student and also employed as a grad student instructor. She reported earning between $40,000 and $59,999 per year. She found out about this project via Twitter. She says that "is funny because I left Twitter... You know how people leave Twitter. And I have a friend who tagged me and was like, 'Girl, this is our time!'" Born and raised in Queens, New York, Gabrielle identifies as a queer bisexual woman. She was eager to participate in this project because "I love *The Golden Girls* so much, so I'm always down to have a conversation about it. But also because [...] finding out, 'Oh, there are other Black people that love this show?' And like, 'I need everyone to know that it makes complete sense for Black people to love the show.' So we need to be up in this study!"

Jasmine found about this project from her best friend, "who is also a *The Golden Girls* enthusiast [...] and she sent [the tweet about the project] to me and I just, 'Oh my gosh, yes! I have to do this.' [...] I was like, 'Anything *The Golden Girls*, I'm there!'" Jasmine, a single, heterosexual female, holds a juris doctorate and works in healthcare law, where she earns more than $100,000 per year. Although she was born in 1988, three years into *The Golden Girls*' original run, she discovered the series via "lots of reruns." Jasmine currently lives in Baltimore and explains, "I come from a single parent household. We have three generations in the house, my grandmother, my mother, and me[....] I was one of those kids that watched whatever the parents were watching[....] If *The Golden Girls* was on, that's what I watched[....] I can't remember a point in life where I wasn't watching *The Golden Girls*."

Jay is a Black gay man who currently lives in Decatur, Georgia. He is single, holds a bachelor's degree, and works in government, where he earns between $75,000 and $99,999 per year. Born in 1978, Jay's favorite Golden Girl is Sophia because he loves "her wit. Like I said, anybody who just comes up with things off the cuff the way she does, I love it. I'm here for it. Now, they all had their little moments, but I think that the way that [Estelle Getty] played that role, she made it everything to me." Jay does not watch many friendcoms. He says, "I did watch *Living Single* when it was on back in the day, but as far as a rerun of it, not really. Never watched *Girlfriends* [UPN, 2000–2006; CW, 2006–2008] like that. Literally, I think *The Golden Girls* is the only show that is a sitcom that stuck with me. Everything else was kind of meh[....] Ain't nothing else have the writing of *The Golden Girls*."

Katherine is a heterosexual, questioning single woman who lives in Portland, Oregon. She was born in 1994, after both *The Golden Girls* and its spinoff *Golden Palace* had concluded. She says, "I feel like there are three shows Black people really love, especially on Twitter. *Frasier* [NBC, 1993–2004], which I also love, *The Golden Girls*, and *Living Single*. And so, once I saw [you were studying] *The Golden Girls* [...] I was like, 'Oh, I really love that show.' And my grandmother recently passed, and she was the one I mainly watched it with." Katherine holds an associate's degree, earns between $25,000 and $39,999 per year working in customer service, and considers herself a fan because "there's a lot of television where I kind of watch something, but not really. I'll maybe watch it once. *The Golden Girls* has been a part of my life for years. It was part of my childhood. It was a part of my teenage life because it used to come on at like 1 a.m. on Logo. So, it became such a big part of my life. I bought merch from the show."

Khadijah earned a PhD and works as a professor in the greater Denver area. She is a heterosexual, single woman who earns more than $100,000 per year. Born in 1975, Khadijah considers herself a *Golden Girls* fan because she has "emotion tied to it because we loved watching that show [as kids]. We would actually tune in on purpose. You look at the *TV Guide*, 'What time is *The Golden Girls* on?' And actually watch it after having seen episodes already—even as reruns. A lot of older shows I've stopped watching like *Three's Company* [ABC, 1977–1984]. But haven't done that with *The Golden Girls*." Khadijah's favorite Golden Girl is Rose because "she's the most pure of heart. She's the one who didn't try to hurt people on purpose. Sometimes even like ... everybody seemed to have their own agenda, whereas Rose didn't seem like she was capable of doing any kind of manipulations."

Born in 1976, **Liz** is a married, college professor who "loved [*The Golden Girls*] instantly." Liz earned a PhD, lives in Takoma Park, Maryland, and makes more than $100,000 each year. Liz, a self-described "mostly straight" woman, was attracted to *The Golden Girls* because in it, she "imagined [her] future self." She says, "I wanted that to be me and my friends. I have two really good friends [. . .] and I remember we would make jokes and say when our husbands are dead or whatever, and we're old and our kids don't want to have anything to do us . . . I remember having this conversation at like 10, 11[. . . .] Like my relationship with my mother is very complicated and not in a positive way. And so it was, for me, like I'd already chosen a chosen family. It's not the vocabulary I would have used then. But now that I look back at my life, it was almost like an escape or imagine like, well, you can choose a family. And then that's the kind of family that I would like. . . that's made of friends and people that you love, and you want to be with. And I just imagine if they could have this great life as older women, that I could too."

Mary's favorite Golden Girl is Sophia because, "I want to be her. Who doesn't want to be Sophia when they get older? Just living the life, and telling it like it is, and being able to grow into having this new family and life. That's who I want to be when I'm older. She's an inspiration." Mary was born in 1988, lives in Oakland, California, with her wife, and identifies as a queer woman. She holds a master's degree and works for a nonprofit company, where she earns between $75,000 and $99,999 per year. Mary's least favorite Golden Girl is Dorothy because "she can be a little self-righteous sometimes. Like I told you, I'm a Dorothy. She's a little too judgmental sometimes."

Megan was born in 1985 and lives with her boyfriend in Atlanta. She earned a bachelor's degree and works in housing and development, where she earns between $40,000 and $59,999 per year. She considers herself a *Golden Girls* fan because "I can recall episodes. I can correlate anything that's going on back to an episode. Me and my friend were on the phone. We both feed off each other when it comes to the episodes of *The Golden Girls*. It's just something that, you know how something becomes a part of you. And you're, 'Oh my God, this is my life!' But when I'm older, this is how I want to be. So I'm a *The Golden Girls* fan, not just a viewer and saying, yeah, I've seen that[. . . .] I've gotten my boyfriend to watch *The Golden Girls* in the morning—and now he's into it, too."

Nick is a single Black gay man who lives in Los Angeles. He found out about this project because one of his good friends "saw your tweet. And I guess he immediately thought of me and sent it to me because he just knows I love *The*

Golden Girls." Born in 1987, Nick has a BFA and works in the entertainment industry where he makes between $40,000 and $59,999 annually. Nick decided to participate in the study because "anything *The Golden Girls* related, I'm like, 'Oh, wow.' And this is like Black, and I'm like, 'Wow! Why not?' That's my jam [. . . .] I did a project in college, and it had nothing to do with *The Golden Girls*, but somehow, I made it about *The Golden Girls*. And this was around the time they had the DVDs, the DVD box and everything. So I took that to class and did a whole presentation about *The Golden Girls* and like the character structure, and it was just fun."

Nikki lives in Concord, Massachusetts, and was born in 1980. She is married, identifies as straight, but also says she is "generally fluid" in terms of her sexuality. At the time of our interview, she was pursuing a master's degree. She works in diversity, equity, and inclusion in education, and earns between $75,000 and $99,999 per year. She believes *The Golden Girls* resonates with Black people because "it touched on topics that were worldly. The core cast was really only [the four Golden Girls] and it felt okay [to not see any people of color] because we never really saw them out in the world, in the sense of going to a coffee shop [. . .] So, I think it felt different because you weren't watching them interact with the world, you were watching a moment in their life [. . . .] and I think honestly, we all have aunts like them, like I have an aunt that can fit into all of these women, and family members, it just felt like family, like people that were really people you would be around."

When meeting new people, **Perdita**, who was born in 1986, uses *The Golden Girls* to gauge who is (and is not) worthy of a friendship. She says, "It's one of those things where like, 'Well, where do you stand on *The Golden Girls*?' [. . .] I remember one person I met, and someone walked past in a *The Golden Girls* T-shirt and I was like, 'Well, that's my show. Me and her could be friends.' And the other person that I was talking to was like, 'Oh, I love *The Golden Girls* and everything.' It's one of those things that's bound to come up in a conversation eventually." Perdita is a single, heterosexual woman who was born in 1986. She earned a bachelor's degree and works in communication. She earns between $40,000 and $59,999 each year and currently resides in Round Rock, Texas.

Qiana earns between $25,000 and $39,999 and at the time of our interview was pursuing a master's degree while also working in communication and public affairs. The Stockton, California, resident found out about this study via Twitter. "Someone I follow liked your post. And it just kind of caught my attention, and I was like, 'I should probably respond.'" Qiana is a single, heterosexual woman and was born in 1986. She says she "vaguely remember[s] childhood, sitting up watching Lifetime with my mom, and it would show *The Golden Girls* and *Designing Women* [CBS, 1986–1993] back-to-back. And so, my afternoons and some evenings on weekends, we would just kind of sit up and watch Lifetime all day. I would watch those shows quite frequently, but I had more of a draw to *The Golden Girls*, and I never quite understood why. My mom thought it was the strangest thing in the world."

Quiniva identifies as a queer lesbian, lives in Brooklyn, and is friends with Gabrielle, whom she informed about this project. She was born in 1993, is single, and holds a juris doctorate. She first started watching *The Golden Girls* as a child and says she loves it because "it's funny as fuck. And I thought it was really funny when I was younger. I think it's really funny now—even when [accounting for] the episodes that haven't aged very well. But I think that I really enjoyed Dorothy and I really enjoyed Blanche as a child, and I attached myself to both of them at a young age." Quiniva earns between $60,000 and $74,999 working in public defense and considers her fandom "loud" because she "took a vacation day from work just to go to the [now closed *Golden Girls*–themed] restaurant [Rue La Rue in New York City]. My friend just gave me, for my birthday, a *The Golden Girls* sleep shirt. We have matching ones [. . . .] I've given out a lot of *The Golden Girls* gifts to people, as well."

Rachel, who lives on Long Island, New York, and was born in 1990, grew up loving Betty White and that led to her love of *The Golden Girls*. She says, "I would just do a deep dive of different things I could watch of Betty White. I would see clips of her on *Mary Tyler Moore Show* [CBS, 1970–1977], and her on *The Golden Girls*. After I finished bingeing *Mary Tyler Moore Show*, my next thing was *The Golden Girls* and I got obsessed that way." When asked why she considers herself a fan and not "just" a *Golden Girls* viewer, the heterosexual, school psychologist says, "I just love quoting *The Golden Girls*. I love talking to one of my coworkers about it, because she's equally as obsessed with it[. . . .] I even have a quarantine mask that is *The Golden Girls*. [. . .] Whenever some of my coworkers or my friends see things about *The Golden Girls*, they send it my way because they're like, 'This is right up your alley. I think you might need to check this out.' One of them actually sent me a link for the mask." Rachel has a postgraduate degree and makes between $60,000 and $74,999 per year.

Racquel lives in Brooklyn and was born in 1980. She holds a PhD and earns more than $100,000 per year. She says, "I remember watching *The Golden*

Girls when it was first airing with my parents, because they were fans of the show[.... W]hen I first watched it with my parents, I thought that the scenarios were funny, just the different situations that they would find themselves." However, the married, heterosexual college professor says "I think the kind of true fandom was when it started running in syndication on Lifetime[....] As I got older, I appreciated that so much of the storylines were driven by their relationships and that there were these throwback things to the characters, and the nature of their personalities. You know, like way that Rose is a dip, but then she'll have these moments of just cutthroat competitiveness, which is the thing that comes up over and over again in the show. So, as I got older, I really liked the dynamic between the women and that it's centered so heavily on their friendship."

Reggie is a single, heterosexual man who was born in 1975 and lives in Detroit where he works as a chaplain, earning more than $100,000 per year. He remembers *The Golden Girls* when it was still producing new episodes. He says, "I didn't search for it, but it was something that ... I heard the first joke, it was between Dorothy and Sophia. And it was just, it was witty. And so, it didn't feel like it was pandering to me. It just felt like it was funny, no matter ... I'm thinking, okay. What if the actresses were Black? Would it be funny? It would still be funny. What if the actresses were same gender loving, it will still be funny. Because it was just absolutely creative and hilarious. And that was enough. It just felt like it would age well. It just felt like it was funny, and it would always be funny, and that drew me." Reggie earned a master's degree and at the time of our interview was pursuing a PhD.

Robin decided to participate in this study because she loves "the idea of Black fandoms. [Black people] will come own it, be a part of the fandom and not have it be, 'Oh, that's a thing that white people like.' I love the idea of normalizing that Black people like things, sort of like my comic books. It doesn't have to be something that is out of the norm for us." Robin was born in 1983 and lives in Washington, DC. She is a single, heterosexual female who works in communication. She holds a master's degree, and at the time of our interview was pursuing a second master's degree. She earns between $75,000 and $99,999 per year. She believes *The Golden Girls* resonates with Black people because the series was "fearless in the topics that they chose to cover, because there are lots of comedies that were way more about a day in the life, the comedy that comes with the ordinary day and it does not necessarily [include] race, validity, discrimination, or the stereotypes that come with being a person of color on television. The Golden Girls approached those episodes, talked about them, and yes, they did joke about them—somewhat problematically sometimes—but they did not shy away from them. I think maybe that's something Black people identify with."

Black Resonance and *The Golden Girls*

It is no newsflash that *Golden Girls* fans, as the category "fan" generally, are always already imagined as white. The scant scholarship on *The Golden Girls* fans and audiences reinforces the whiteness of the series' imagined fan base by centering its particular import for white gay communities.[14] My white husband recalls that on Saturday nights at 9 p.m. EST the now-defunct Washington, DC, gay nightclub Mr. P's would turn off the music so its queer patrons could watch the newest episode of *The Golden Girls*. When we met and discovered that we shared *Golden Girls* fandom, I never attributed my love for "The Girls" to my Blackness, thinking that perhaps only folks who were queer *and* Black loved *The Golden Girls*. Similarly, Black *Golden Girls* fan Aaron, 49, New York City, says, "I never would have thought of myself as a Black fan of *The Golden Girls* or that there would even be a group of Black fans of *The Golden Girls* [. . .] I have a very diverse circle of friends, but I don't have any discussions with any of them, none of the ones who are Black even bring up *The Golden Girls*." Like Aaron, I was surprised that Black folks (many of whom did not identify as LGBTQIA) considered themselves *Golden Girls* fans, particularly because, as the other case studies in this book attest, Black fandom is rarely rooted in joy centrally, but joy *and* some sort of activist use of the Black look.

The nexus of this chapter's exploration of Black fandom and *The Golden Girls* is twofold. First, in the age of social media, Black folks began taking up, reworking, and remixing *The Golden Girls* to reflect a Black experience more closely. Perhaps most famously, YouTube content creator Aaron Scott's 2016 video "The Golden Girls Gospel Remix (Full Song)" took *The Golden Girls'* theme song and resignified it into a gospel-tinged call-and-response video that has amassed more than 6 million views and turned him into a viral sensation.[15] Similarly, TikTok user @marvinhoward produced a video called "The Black Golden Girls" in which he and user

Figure 4.3. Still from the establishing shot of "The Black Golden Girls," which lovingly refashions the series as one situated within Blackness.

@PattyMayonaze enact an opening credit sequence that resets the original Miami-based series in a decidedly more "urban" space. The video's establishing shot features Popeyes Chicken and TJ Maxx and is accompanied by Scott's "Blackened" version of the theme song.[16] These resignifications of *The Golden Girls* expose how, as race and technology scholar Sarah Florini posits, "Black fans create parallel culturally resonant fan practices that mitigate their erasure not only from fandom but also from many of their beloved media texts."[17] These remixes demonstrate the resonance *The Golden Girls* has for some Black people such that they become textual poachers, taking bits and pieces of a beloved text and reshaping it to fit their needs, but always centering their affection for the series.[18]

Second, Black celebrities began more loudly proclaiming their love for the series. In her 2017 appearance on *Hot Ones* (YouTube, 2015–present), actress Gabrielle Union asked host Sean Evans, "Did you know that [rapper] DMX loves *The Golden Girls*? That's a real fun fact." When asked how she knew that, she said, "Because he watches it in his trailer" and once invited her to watch with him because, he explained, "shit is funny."[19] Additionally, on September 8, 2020, Black actresses Tracee Ellis Ross, Regina King, Alfre Woodard, and Sanaa Lathan participated in a table read of the *Golden Girls* episode "Flu Attack" to inform and educate about voting rights and encourage Black people to complete the census as part of the Zoom series "Zoom Where It Happens."[20] These two occurrences point to the series' resonance among Black people: in the case of DMX, "coming out" as a Black *Golden Girls* fan when working with Union on *Cradle 2 the Grave* (2003, dir. Andrzej Bartkowiak). In the second case, understanding that *The Golden Girls* coupled with the specific Black actresses performing the roles would attract Black viewers to advance a social justice aim.

The description of the event read:

> Join us for an evening that takes a look back to the sitcoms of yesteryear-Before you could pause your screens or binge watch. We bring to you our

Figure 4.4. Image from the first "Zoom Where It Happens" featuring a *Golden Girls* episode with Black actresses Regina King, Sanaa Lathan, Alfre Woodard, and Tracee Ellis Ross as "The Girls."

rendition of Golden Girls, reimagined with an all-black cast of your favorite actresses: Alfre Woodard, Tracee Ellis Ross, Sanaa Lathan, and Regina King, directed by Gina Prince-Bythewood and hosted by Lena Waithe.

In an effort to further engage our community and drive change, all you need to do to enjoy this evening is sign up to receive messages about how you can make a change during this election!

This event is in partnership with Zoom, and the first episode is spotlighting and supporting Color of Change—the nation's largest online racial justice organization.

We'll see you Tuesday, in Zoom Where it Happens.

With respect to the reception of the *Golden Girls* Zoom reading, some Black Twitter users (identified as such by their avatar) were excited about Black actresses taking over the roles of Dorothy, Blanche, Rose, and Sophia. One Black-presenting Twitter user, @DocAshBattle, declared that the "reading of the *Golden Girls* [was] a mash up on [her] favorite things: Black People & the *Golden Girls*." Black Twitter user @dharman69 said, "Oh man, this did my heart so good! [. . .] I was mouthing the dialogue right along with [the actresses]. Thank you for being our friends tonight."[21] These Black Twitter users demonstrate the series' resonance among some Black folks and a willingness to "Blacken" a beloved text, somewhat like Black-cast films of the 1970s like *Blacula* (1972, dir. William Crain), *Blackenstein* (1973, dir. William A. Levey), and *The Wiz* did. However, some Black Twitter users wanted the series left alone, without feeling the need to reboot and/or "Blacken" the series to give it meaning for Black fans. As media scholar Kristen Warner theorizes, Black resonance is not always concerned with seeing Black bodies and/or having Black bodies shout their Blackness from the media rooftops.[22] For example, Black Twitter user @TheRastaEmpress proclaimed, "I don't need a *The Golden Girls* remake. Leave the classic ALONE."[23] While contradictory, both sets of reading responses detail how *The Golden Girls*, in its original iteration, resonated with Black audiences—although there was nothing explicit in the text that hailed Black fans representationally. Rather, *The Golden Girls* activates "affective elements of consciousness and relationships" for Black fans and, in so doing, provides them with comfort.[24]

The Golden Girls, Openness, and Comfort

As a television series that originated squarely within the network era, a period in which original television content was aired mainly on the "Big 3" networks (ABC, CBS, and NBC), *The Golden Girls* needed to attempt to capture as large an audience share as possible for survival. While contemporarily series with audiences in the 5 million viewer range can survive for seasons, the network era was marked by shows that media scholar Janet Staiger calls "Blockbuster TV" because they routinely captured the eyeballs of at least one out of every three television viewers.[25] In its premiere episode, *The Golden Girls* attracted 21.5 million viewers and its series finale attracted 17.4 million.[26] As such, *The Golden Girls*, and its openness as a text for a number of different audience segments, is worth exploring, particularly its Black viewership in light of the infrequency with which the series featured Black actors/characters.

When I invoke openness, what I mean is that if someone says, "Make yourself comfortable," as you enter their home, their home is open to you and that you have been welcomed in it (presuming they are sincere). Part of the comfort Black *Golden Girls* fans find in the series, is that it is an open and polysemic text.[27] Like the notion of making a guest feel comfortable in one's home, the openness of a media text similarly welcomes a viewer to interpret the text in myriad ways that will help them find comfort and enjoyment in it. *The Golden Girls*, thus, had to seek a big, broad audience to ensure its survival for seven seasons, and its openness is one of the ways Black fans found, and continue to find, comfort in it.

Alba, 46, Harlem, New York, suggests that *The Golden Girls* feels open to her because it "doesn't really alienate anybody [. . .]. So even though they were older, and I was definitely *not* the target demo, it made getting older a goal. You hear women saying like, 'Well I'm just going to get older and just move into a house with my friends.'" Alba felt welcomed into *The Golden Girls* because, while it did not necessarily hail her, she did not feel prohibited from trying to enter *The Golden Girls*. At the same time, in its openness to her, it allowed her to read the series as aspirational. In other words, for Alba, because the series was open to her, it gave her a blueprint for aging—one that looked decidedly different from the ways older women had been previously mediated within television. Ashlée, 38, Louisville, Kentucky, adds that *The Golden Girls* resonates for her partly because her maternal grandmother died when she was young, and she does not have close patrilineal relationships. She finds resonance and comfort in *The Golden Girls* because, she says, "I was always missing like a grandmother. 'The Girls,' I think I connected to them because of that." For Ashlée, the series' openness, and thus comfort, is in how it allows her to map a fictional relationship onto these "grandmotherly" characters in the absence of a real-life relationship. For both Alba and Ashlée, their relationship to the series and its characters crosses racial boundaries.

The openness of the series and the ways it centered female friendship allowed a "way in" for Black *Golden Girls* fans. Chris, 35, Waco, Texas, describes how *The Golden Girls* resonates for her:

> It's the community and those types of friendships [in the show], because I feel like, just in a way that Black women . . . I'll speak from a Black female perspective, sometimes when you're happy, you call your friends, "Bitch, let me tell you . . ." and I think that kind of, that way of relating and the playful teasing and, I think that probably mimics a lot of my friendships with Black women. And I have a lot of white friends and I think that the way that I relate to Black women is different. The way we tease each other and treat each other, I think that I see those kinds of friendships in *The Golden Girls* as opposed to the way I relate to my white friends.

While the series had only one Black female writer (Winifred Hervey), the friendships felt different, and perhaps more resonant for Black fans (and Black women fans in particular), because of how they related to one another. Gabrielle, 31, Pittsburgh, says that although *The Golden Girls* is filled with white characters, she and her boyfriend have decided "it really makes sense for *The Golden Girls* to register culturally [for Black people], I think, because in a lot of ways it's just like playing the dozens. It's just like this sense that you can love your friend deeply, but also loathe them." Both Chris and Gabrielle illuminate how *The Golden Girls* puts an affectively racialized twist on friendship. In other words, while "The Girls" were not Black, they *felt* Black. While Chris does not specifically mention the dozens, "a mode of street-smart verbal jousting [mostly] affiliated with urban, working-class, super-masculine (i.e., avowedly heterosexual) African-American culture since at least the early 20th century," both she and Gabrielle decode the mix of love and verbal sparring among the residents of 6151 Richmond Street within Black structures of meaning and feeling.[28] The openness of *The Golden Girls* allows these fans to access the series and filter it through their own experiences in order to find comfort within it.

Home, Family, and Thematic Representation

Black fans connect the comfort they find in viewing *The Golden Girls* to be partly about the notion of home. Television historian Lynn Spigel detailed how, since the middle of the 20th century, television and the home had a cozy and symbiotic relationship, with the TV set becoming the architectural and entertainment center of the home's public sphere.[29] That, as a child Black *Golden Girls* fan, I allowed Dorothy, Sophia, Rose, and Blanche into my family's home every Saturday night or that contemporary viewers can call up "The Girls" "on demand" are examples of how some Black fans' relationship to the series is structured.

In addition to home as an architectural component of the television set and television viewing, structurally, *The Golden Girls* is not *just* a sitcom—but a *domestic* sitcom (or domesticom), which means the primary "action" in the series is confined to the home. Like most multi-camera sitcoms, *The Golden Girls* has two primary sets: (1) the kitchen, where "The Girls" often congregate to enjoy cheesecake and a coffee klatch; and (2) the living room. Within the fantasy of the domestic comedy, the lines between friend and family are often blurred. By the very nature of its homeboundness, the domesticom makes a family of its main characters whether they are related by bloodlines or via friendships. These friendships can often *feel* like family. In fact, in *The Golden Girls*' series finale, Dorothy centers "The Girls" as family as she is leaving 6151 Richmond Street to begin her life with her new husband. The last line of dialogue is Dorothy tearfully telling Blanche, Rose, and Sophia, "You'll always be my sisters. Always." *The Golden Girls* in its finale (as well as at various times throughout the series) thus uses the domestic sitcom to rework the definition of the televisual family. And if, as media scholar Jonathan Gray argues, the domestic sitcom serves "as a prime huckster selling the American Dream and its related notions

Figure 4.5. Rose, Dorothy, and Blanche enjoy cheesecake and conversation while Sophia looks on in the background. As one of *The Golden Girls*' two main sets, the kitchen centers its concerns as almost entirely domestic.

of family, home, and suburb," the comfort found in *The Golden Girls* transcodes and rearticulates what precisely both "home" and "family" mean.[30] In other words, the "American Dream" to which many other sitcoms gestured was different than the lived realities of some Black Americans. Many Black folks have lived among extended family and alternative kinship networks often because the very white mediated ideal of the "American Dream" was not available to us. We often *had* to live in these arrangements for financial reasons, much like Blanche, Rose, Dorothy, and Sophia.

For Black fans, the series resonated partly because it allowed them to map themselves and/or their family onto the broader character archetypes. Brooke, 39, Grand Rapids, Michigan, says she sees "The Girls" in her "own family. I can see my Aunt T in Blanche and my cousin in Rose." While Charles, 48, Philadelphia, doesn't necessarily see his family in the series, as a Black pansexual man, he says, "I find myself in the characters. I wish I had the opportunity to be part of something that perfect." For Black fans like Brooke and Charles, *The Golden Girls*, as a white-cast sitcom, allows them to eschew racial representation and substitute it for what I am calling thematic representation. That is, Black fans look for themes and characterizations that resonate rather than looking for images that resemble them. Thematic representation works across race, gender, and sexual orientation such that men, Black folks, and members of LGBTQIA communities can all find thematic representations within *The Golden Girls* resonant enough to take up the series as a fan object. The series' openness and universality engenders a transracial fannish experience for Black fans.

Dorcia, 40, Fairfield County, Connecticut, says:

> Although there weren't any recurring roles for Black people, I think the characters were fully developed enough that any person can identify with them. Like they weren't like white characters, because I haven't really watched any, now that I think about it, I never really watched *Friends* [NBC, 1994–2004], I never watched *Seinfeld* [NBC, 1989–1998] or any of those shows where there weren't Black people. I tend not to watch them, but *The Golden Girls*, I think it, and this might sound like a little hokey, but maybe because I feel like it transcended race. Sophia, even though she's Sicilian, I could easily see her being one of my friend's grandmothers. Blanche I could definitely see being, even though she's so Southern and even conservative, I could still see her being an auntie.

Dorcia makes a distinction between other white-cast sitcoms like *Friends* and *Seinfeld* and *The Golden Girls*. While all three sitcoms are united by the whiteness of their cast, and they could even be united by ethnicity (New York Jewishness in *Seinfeld* and *Friends* and New York Italianness in *The Golden Girls*), *The Golden Girls'* openness as a text allows for a reading of Dorothy, Rose, Blanche, and Sophia that, while it does not make them Black characters, makes them *feel* Black. Black *Golden Girls* fans, in the absence of racial representation, focus on thematic representation through the series' relationships and character traits that might connect to their broader lives. In other words, Black *Golden Girls* fans find comfort in *feeling* seen in the absence of *being* seen through explicit Black representation. When they cannot *see* Blackness explicitly, shows like *The Golden Girls* allows them to *feel* Black themes.

For Black *Golden Girls* fans, the series' openness also allows them to understand life paths that may not always conform to hegemonic ideals about family. Because many of the Black *Golden Girls* fans I interviewed were much younger than Dorothy, Rose, Blanche, and Sofia at the time they became fans, many, at least retrospectively, use *The Golden Girls* to imagine their own futures. For example, Chris, 35, Waco, Texas, says, "I was a fat girl [. . .] I was well aware of like my . . . how being fat effects your [perceived] desirability. And so, I was kind of like, 'Okay, well, I don't know if I'll get married or anything like that, but, like this is a way of seeing women on TV. I have friends and then maybe I could grow old and just be happy with a bunch of my friends.'" Ashlée, 38, Louisville, Kentucky, deepens this idea by saying *The Golden Girls* allows her to imagine the "whole idea of a chosen family." She continues:

> Now granted I didn't know that I was bisexual when I was 20, right? [. . .] I mean, granted society didn't reject them or anything like that [like often happens with queer people], but the fact that they chose to be more than roommates. They chose to be friends and family and they said that over and over again. "We are a family. We are here for one another." [. . .] I think especially when you identify as queer in some way that the idea of chosen families is really important as well. People that you see your full self with, you know?"

The Golden Girls engages a notion of chosen family for some Black fans that allows them to imagine "family" that may not resemble how "family" is often depicted in sitcoms—particularly ones as popular as *The Golden Girls*. Enabling "alternative" representational and dialogic practices, *The Golden Girls* allows Black fans like Chris to imagine her Black, fat, female body as belonging to a family, and for Ashlée to see a way for her proto-queer self to imagine family in ways that do not resemble hegemonic definitions of the term.

As a component of comfort, ideals about extended family and the home structure how Black *Golden Girls* fans decode the series. From the notion of mapping familial and personal relationships onto the characters to imagining futures that look less like a "traditional" family, *The Golden Girls*' openness allows Black fans to find comfort within its narrative universe. And that comfort transcends racial boundaries. For

Black *Golden Girls* fans, the series is unlike most other white-cast sitcoms in that they feel welcomed in by the text rather than alienated by its whiteness. In "The Girls'" rearticulation of family, *The Golden Girls* feels resonant as a way for Black fans to see their current and future family formations depicted. And for them, that feels comforting.

Familiarity and/as Comfort

The return to a beloved object is often rooted in how it provides pleasure. For many Black *Golden Girls* fans, the series' pleasure can be partly located in its familiarity, a familiarity engendered through repeated viewing. Feminist scholar Susanna Paasonen helps make the connection between resonance and comfort clear when she argues that the aim of resonance is not simply to hold the viewer's attention and fascinate them. Rather, texts that resonate require repeated consumption.[31] This repeated consumption, enabled by the series' availability in syndication, on DVD, and via streaming platforms, allows Black *Golden Girls* fans to watch the series whenever they like and, as such, it can "achieve an indelible place in everyday routines."[32] The routinization of *The Golden Girls* is evident in the assertion by Perdita, 37, Round Rock, Texas, that:

> I've consistently watched, I guess, from 11 or so to maybe 14, 15, or maybe a little bit older, and then I went into the Navy, and then I picked [*The Golden Girls*] back up I guess around 19–20, and I have consistently watched it from that age on to the present. And I bought the DVDs because I realized [. . .] I can come in at night, I can put on an episode of *The Golden Girls* and it's like catching up with old friends[. . . .] So when I sit up and I watch them all together, and I've seen these episodes hundreds of times by this time, I can do whatever around the house, stop and watch a few minutes and laugh like I've never seen this episode before, and then going about my business. Or if I'm tired and I just need to chill, I can put it on and I can decompress. There's a constant level of comfort that I have with that show.

Perdita suggests that she has a fictional relationship with "The Girls" in her admission that watching the series feels like connecting with friends. For her, that allows a simultaneous sense of decompression and pleasure.

But it is also her mastery of the series (having seen episodes "hundreds of times") that allows her to work *The Golden Girls* into her routine. She can go "about her business" without giving the series 100 percent of her attention but periodically check in with "The Girls" and continue to find joy and comfort in watching.

Similarly, Qiana, 30, New York City, says, "I'm just grateful that streaming is the thing now, so I don't have to worry about recording on VHS to watch [. . .] it whenever I want. [. . .] I think knowing I can turn to [*The Golden Girls*] for comfort anytime I'm feeling down . . . If I'm in a bad mood, who's going to make me feel better? It's probably going to be a *Golden Girls* situation." Qiana points to the ways her mastery of the series also means that she knows *The Golden Girls* can lift her mood. And because the program is available via streaming, she can always use it to lift her spirits, rather than having to wait for it to be broadcast via linear television. Thus, for Perdita and Qiana, part of *The Golden Girls'* Black resonance is in the notion that it provides them comfort. Perdita works the series into her daily routine and Qiana checks in with "The Girls" when she needs a pick-me-up.

Often the familiarity Black fans associate with the comfort *The Golden Girls* provides is centered on the memories they attach to the series. In other words, while these Black fans undoubtedly love the series, that love is intertwined with often familial memories. Jasmine, 35, Baltimore, says *The Golden Girls* is:

> just as much a part of me as being in Baltimore and being with my mother. I can call her at any given moment that [*The Golden Girls*] is on either Hallmark or TV Land, and I'm like, "What are you doing?" And she's like, "Watching *The Golden Girls*." If nothing else, it's a go-to. I used to remember early in the morning when I would be home when I had my daughter, she's been seeing *The Golden Girls* since she came home from the hospital, because it came on early in the morning and I was up, I would have it on for those couple of hours[. . . .] It is just a part of me.

For Jasmine, the series connects her to two generations of Black women/girls: her mother and her daughter. This intergenerational fandom is a kind of pedagogy that works like *The Wiz*'s Black fandom explored in chapter 3. The text carries import for Jasmine's family's internal "culture." Jasmine's *Golden Girls* "structures of feeling" are concerned "with meanings and values as they are actively lived and felt" as she engages with the series.[33] Those meanings and values cultural theorist Raymond Williams finds central to his theorization of structures of feeling also shape the engagement of Katherine, 29, Portland, Oregon. She says, "I just have more of [an] emotional reaction [to *The Golden Girls*] because I have so many memories of watching that show with people or interacting with that show." Both Jasmine's and Katherine's ongoing connections to *The Golden Girls* are affectively tethered to those relationships. Their repeated viewing of the series is certainly connected to their enjoyment of the show on its own merits. However, the relationships they recall when engaging with *The Golden Girls* heighten the experience of watching and help solidify their fandom.

At the same time, the familiarity associated with comfort is often found in the simple act of repeated viewing. As Alba, 46, Harlem, New York, says:

> I am the person who watches *The Golden Girls* every night because again, comforting. I don't know. I never thought about this until I spoke to you, but [. . .] to go to bed, I need something on. And so, I turn *The Golden Girls* on because I don't have to watch it to see it, because I know every episode. You show me the beginning and I'm like, "Oh this is the episode where you get X, Y, and Z."

Similarly, Nick, 36, Los Angeles, says, "At some point in my life, it's turned from just like, 'oh, watch it every now and then,' to like, 'I have to have it, I have to watch it, I have to see it, I have to put it on when I go to sleep.' It just became a part of my life." Alba and Nick find the series so comforting that they both can fall asleep with it on. And importantly, it is their *choice* of *The Golden Girls* over any other of the endless possibilities of media content that might soothe them that sets the series apart from others. The level of comfort they find in *The Golden Girls* is rooted in their knowledge of the series such that they can fall asleep during it without missing any pertinent narrative points—or at least ones that they would miss if they were unfamiliar with the text.

Charles, 48, Philadelphia, finds similar comfort in repeatedly watching *The Golden Girls*. He describes the show as being "like comfort food. I have my Bluetooth shower speaker and I just put on episodes of *The Golden Girls* to play while I'm taking a shower just because it's comforting. I know it's there and I know the jokes that don't have to see it." Part of the comfort Charles find in repeatedly viewing *The Golden Girls* is its predictability. In some senses, Alba, Nick, and Charles point to how their mastery of *The Golden Girls* allows them to treat it as almost background noise. However, it is not that Alba, Nick, or Charles ignore the show when they have chosen to play it. Rather, they know the text so well that it becomes like a warm blanket that Nick and Alba can wrap themselves inside until slumber comes, or a warm shower that prepares Charles for his day.

A final aspect of the ways *The Golden Girls* engenders familiarity and comfort among its Black fans is how it helps them understand friendships and relationships. For example, Racquel, 43, New York City, recalled that, on their first date, her now-husband teased her about her *Golden Girls* fandom. She joked that a second date almost did not happen because of that teasing. In other words, Racquel used her fandom to figure out if someone was worthy of her time. In her suggestion that her date did not take *The Golden Girls* seriously, she details (albeit jokingly, considering that they eventually married) the ways affection for the series functions as a shorthand to understand new people. Those who like *The Golden Girls* are automatically understood as "good." Those who do not like the series are questionable as friends and partners. Similarly, Robin, 40, Washington, DC, recalls starting a new job and "breaking the ice" by telling her new co-workers about her love for *The Golden Girls*. "I said, one of my favorite things to do when I'm relaxing is watch *The Golden Girls* episodes. A lot of people were like, 'Oh yeah, I love that show!' That's been kind of my fun fact whenever I introduce myself to new people." She continues by saying that while she does not find it odd that someone might not have seen the show, "I would think they're suspect if they didn't like the show or they didn't find anybody to identify with, because I'm like, 'There's a little bit of everything on this show. Everybody gets along. If you don't see anything on this show that you like or can identify with, then I'm going to look at you suspect.'" Ultimately, then, affective responses to *The Golden Girls* helps some Black fans, like

Figure 4.6. A Facebook exchange between Racquel and her husband about her *Golden Girls* fandom and how she uses the series to gauge romantic relationships.

Racquel and Robin, structure other relationships and determine whether or not those relationships are worthy of further exploration. In short, the familiarity of *The Golden Girls* and its attendant fandom is simultaneously connected to the comfort Black fans think they will find in new people they encounter. If a new potential friend or partner is a *Golden Girls* fan, there might be possibility for the relationship. If they are not, then how the relationship develops is more of a question in their minds.

Welcome to the Comfort Zone: Blackness and *The Golden Girls*

Black *Golden Girls* fandom is not entirely disconnected from how class is related to Misty Copeland and canon is related to *The Wiz*. *The Golden Girls* is particularly distinguished from other white-cast sitcoms like *Friends* and *Seinfeld* as speaking more centrally to how Black fans seek comfort through white-cast media in ways similar to how Black fans make a classed choice wanting Misty Copeland in American Ballet Theatre instead of the fictional Wichita Ballet Theatre. And in that selection of *The Golden Girls* over *Friends* or *Seinfeld*, Black fans also elevate *The Golden Girls* as canonical through the ways they use dialogue from the series in their everyday lives, like Potluck does with *The Wiz*. In short, there are ways that Black fandom works similarly with Black-cast media *and* white-cast media.

Black *Golden Girls* fandom demonstrates that, when the politics of visibility have been replaced with a politics of resonance, fans can find joyful fandom. Unlike some of the ways Black fans take up Misty Copeland, *Black Panther*, and *The Wiz*, when Black bodies are absent, there is no need to make Black viewing political. There is also little desire for a reboot of *The Golden Girls* that might recast the series with Black actors like the second adaptation of *Uncle Buck* (ABC, 2016) with a Black cast. Ultimately, such a move would activate a politics of representation that is absent when it is "just" four old white ladies sharing a home together in Miami. In *The Golden Girls*, Black fans find Black joy. *The Golden Girls* allows Black fans to finally let their hair down and simply enjoy the antics of Dorothy Zbornak, Rose Nylund, Blanche Devereaux, and Sofia Petrillo at 6151 Richmond Street in Miami in comfort.

Black fans do not necessarily have a desire to join a larger *Golden Girls* fan community. While many of the Black fans owned T-shirts, board games, and other tchotchkes that they purchased or received as gifts, their fandom was most closely associated with the comfort of the text itself. Perhaps some of that is rooted in the noted anti-Blackness (and quite frankly, anti-anything not white and male) that often structures fan communities.[34] None of the Black fans reported that they went to *Golden Girls* trivia events, had seen drag performances of episodes, or had done *Golden Girls* pub crawls. Only one Black *Golden Girls* fan (Ashlée) attended Golden Con, a *Golden Girls* fan convention that was first held in Chicago in April 2022. And attending the Golden Girls Kitchen in both New York and Chicago, I saw very few Black fans in attendance. While there may certainly be an economic component to Black *Golden Girls* fans' structuring their fandom only through the series, I suggest that it is more closely associated with the ways Black fans want to experience the series from the comfort of their own homes. There is certainly a love of the series, but that love is connected to the ways *The Golden Girls* feels familiar, how it mediates alternative kinship formations, and its engendering of nostalgic feelings. In a word, *The Golden Girls* is comfort TV for the Black fan's soul.

Conclusion

Fandom for Us

As I prepared to write this conclusion, the US Supreme Court had just ruled that affirmative action was no longer needed to ensure inclusion and equality in institutions of higher learning.[1] Given the continued rightward march in United States politics, higher education will not be the only place where the gains Black folks made in the immediate wake of the 1960s Civil Rights Movement will eventually be eroded by those aggrieved white people who "lost something" when Black folks got closer to being treated as humans. In American culture, the belief is that access cannot expand for those excluded without other folks "losing" something—remember when white folks felt they needed to "take the country back" when Barack Obama was elected president? And yet, here we are again with the haves getting more and the have-nots continuing to be excluded from participation in the so-called American Dream. So Black folks wonder, like the lyrics from "Home" from *The Wiz* ask, "should we try and stay, or should we run away, or will it be better just to let things be?" And even as we have racial battle fatigue mixed with Black rage, we decide to stay and fight. And one of the fronts on which the fight continues is through the politics of our Black look—that is, we use our Black gaze to consume, advocate for, and celebrate Blackness.

Fandom for Us, by Us demonstrates the ways Black fan practices fuse representation, reception, consumerism, pleasure, and activism. That fusion is rooted in a form of neoliberal consumer activism that centers capitalist logics to ensure inclusion and visibility. Put another way, while Black fandom chooses its own objects, it chooses those objects with an eye toward assimilation. By fashioning ourselves as good consumer citizens, we hope to finally be granted a seat at the mainstream table. Because, as media scholar Herman Gray avers, "media remain the crucial site where different sectors of disenfranchised populations and communities continue to seek [. . .] recognition and greater visibility as a measure of cultural justice and social equality," Black folks retain their investment in Black mediated images.² This reliance on visibility and inclusion is, in many ways, understood as the endgame; to be seen by/for a white mainstream is to be included, at long last, in the imagination of what it means to be an American. But, Black fandom is simultaneously an act of resistance, an act of supplication, and a rejection of mainstream taste cultures. Thus, Black folks use class, clout, canon, and comfort to get themselves closer to the mountaintop Martin Luther King, Jr., hoped America would one day achieve.

The Black look is not passive. The Black look does not simply allow messages to be passively injected into our veins. Rather, the Black look picks and chooses which content it lets in, takes on, and heralds as worthy. In chapter 1, I detailed the ways that *class*, as a Black fannish practice, describes how Black fans distinguish between what they understand as "worthy" and "unworthy" fan objects. Those distinctions are made by using taste to elevate, for example, American Ballet Theatre (ABT) above the fictional Wichita Ballet Theatre (WBT). ABT is configured as "better" than WBT because of the politics inherent in its naming—ABT is, as President Obama's designation attests, "America's National Ballet Company," whereas WBT belongs "only" to Wichita. Thus, Misty Copeland is elevated as a Black fan object because she has not only excelled in a historically white (and racist) artform, but because she has done so in "America's National Ballet Company." And that Black excellence, alongside her having "broken the barrier" as the first Black woman to be promoted to the rank of principal dancer at ABT, makes her a suitable role model for Black children. Concomitantly, seeing her #BlackExcellence on display—and having other folks of all races also have to see and reckon with her Black body in motion boldly taking up space—is an act of Black joy.

Chapter 2 engaged the ways Black fans positioned *Black Panther* as a Black-cast film that could instill pride in their Black children. T'Challa and other characters like his sister, Shuri, were not simply configured as good role models; Black fans used their *clout* as consumers to signal to the broader media industries that if they invest in high-budget, "high-quality" Black-cast content, then Black audiences will use their clout to support such content. That clout is used to distinguish between media texts like *Black Panther* and, for example, *Acrimony* (2018, dir. Tyler Perry). While they each activated must-see Blackness in varying ways, the comparatively small budget for *Acrimony* ($20 million) compared to *Black Panther*'s ($200 million) meant that Black fans understood the stakes of failure differently. *Black Panther* truly could not fail because of how that failure would be mapped onto the industrial viability of Black audiences and fans. Clout, as a Black fan practice, is thus keenly aware of and interested in Black futurity. When a text like *Black Panther* emerges, Black folks "do it for the culture" even as they often find enjoyment in the consumption. But the exercise of their clout is the main thing that carries import. It demands more visibility and viability of Black talent by making the visibility and viability of Black audiences known. And yet, exercising this clout was joyous. Seeing Blackness projected on 50-foot screens bought Black people pride. We saw the "regalness" of Blackness that is often denied us when we watch slave narratives. Where television and film properties like *Roots* (ABC, 1977) depict Africa as "primitive" in order to make slavery seem like it "civilized" Black folks, *Black Panther* showed us as kings and queens.

Whereas chapters 1 and 2 mostly centered the work of the Black look, chapter 3 shifted to more explicitly engaging Black joy in Black fan practices. Examining the process of Black *canon* formation reveals the joy Black fans derive from creating a living, breathing archive of beloved Black objects that resonate. Black fans are ambivalent about the "goodness" or "badness" of canonized objects as much as they are concerned with how the objects feel Black. These Black objects are canonized because, like the first song in *The Wiz*, Black folks do not want to "lose the feeling that we have" around specific objects. And canonized objects, like *The Wiz*, are "passed down" because they carry import for generations of Black fans and also serve a socializing function between Black generations. Black canon objects become part of a Black lexicon that indexes objects not necessarily because they are "good," but because they are concomitantly deemed important *and* affective. That import and affective attachment manifests in how Black fans use and reuse Black canonical objects in their everyday life through language and collective memory.

Lastly, chapter 4 doubled down on Black joy by looking at Black fandom of *The Golden Girls*. Black folks found comfort in *The Golden Girls* in a way they do not in, say, *Friends* (NBC, 1994–2004) because they can see themselves and their families depicted in *The Golden Girls* even through its whiteness. Black fandom is not necessarily about representation mattering, but about the matter of resonance, and how Black fans can deploy that resonance to make the mediated world and the world Black folks inhabit everyday a better place. These two things do not stand in opposition to one another. Rather, there are in a dialectical relationship in which representation matters precisely because it resonates.

Black Fandom as Universal (and Particular)

Fandom for Us, by Us, as I argued in the introduction, is a political project that has deliberately centered Black fan practices. As I also gestured toward in the introduction, these fan practices are not wholly Black fan practices, but are, instead, fan practices that Black people do. I imagine that many white scholars doing their white fandom work will dismiss the findings in *Fandom for Us, by Us* as so specifically about Blackness as to have no value for their work on whiteness (even as they ignore that they are talking about whiteness and position the invisibility of whiteness as "universal"). Yet, while I insist on the particularity of Blackness, I also equally insist that Blackness can simultaneously be every bit as universal as whiteness within research.

For example, the ways and the reasons fans take up a fan object are rooted in *class*. Similar to how Black fans chose and elevated Misty Copeland as a fan object, media scholars Cornell Sandvoss, Jonathan Gray, and C. Lee Harrington argue that "rock fans lambast pop music fans in a move that is [. . .] based upon a desire to place rock above pop in a cosmic hierarchy of musical genres."[3] In other words, all fandoms, including white fandoms, Black fandoms, Asian fandoms, and Latinx fandoms, are concerned with the elevation of one fan object choice at the expense of others. Black fans elevate Copeland over other Black dancers in modern dance and more "local"-sounding ballet companies (like New York City Ballet or the Joffrey Ballet of Chicago) because being a Black woman who "willed what she wanted" and became a principal dancer with "America's National Ballet Company" works to position Copeland as being in a class by herself and worthy of fandom. However, what makes Copeland's fandom Black is how the choice and heralding of

Copeland are enmeshed in a politic that positions her as unique. She is *not* a modern dance, tap, or jazz dancer, fields that have historically welcomed and celebrated Black dancers. She broke a barrier, but it was not without its own trauma. In a 2024 interview with journalist Chris Wallace, Copeland said, "I spent the first decade of my professional career with American Ballet Theatre, the only Black woman in the company—a company of almost 100 dancers [. . .] I've experienced, you know, difficulties being a Black woman when you stand out, especially in the corps de ballet when it's supposed to look uniform, and everyone kind of in the same tones wearing pink tights, which represent the color of your skin. And that wasn't always the case."[4] Thus, Copeland's Black fandom champions her as a show of lifting her up externally while she works internally within a primarily white space and artform. She is chosen by Black fans because she chose to make Blackness visible in a space they had not seen Blackness before.

White "nerds" have long used their fandom to make themselves visible as a viable market segment. In 2017, fan studies scholar Henry Jenkins observed that fan cultures were predicted to have "a real economic and cultural impact; where fan tastes are ruling at the box office [. . .] where fan tastes are dominating television [. . . and] where fan practices are shaping the games industry."[5] In short, fans understand their industrial *clout*. They believe that their eyeballs, the very act of their looking, can shape what gets produced across film, television, and gaming cultures. For Black fans, clout is used in much the same way. The Black fandom use of clout is similarly bound within futurity. Like "nerd" fandoms, Black fans use clout to try to connect spectatorship and consumer spending to production practices. Concomitantly, Black fandom sutures the politics of the Black look to a broader Black culture. Black fandoms are engaged "for the culture" writ large *and* for the ways images structure a Black future—"good" Black media images give Black children "positive" role models to prop up their self-esteem in a fundamentally racist and anti-Black world.

All fandoms create *canon*. However, in much of the fandom literature, canon is described as simply the work as it was fashioned by its creators. Canon, then, as far as fandom studies is concerned, is most interested in creating a "base" from which fans can create a participatory body of work that expands and reshapes the text creators created.[6] Where canon shifts within Black canon is in the latter's attention to a set of particular Black texts that are resonant for Black fans. It certainly takes the text as fashioned by its creators, but it centers Blackness and Black productions that are imagined as being important "for the culture" and elevates them beyond just "regular" Black-cast texts. Canon is less interested in reshaping the text to fit fan needs and/or correct plot lines or characters. It is also less interested in making aesthetic or narrative judgements about the text. Rather, Black canon is invested in Black feeling, which is always already bound within a centering of Black value(s). That is, these Black feelings result in Black fans sharing valuable Black cultural texts across generations of Black folks. Black canon is interested in the ways these texts get used and reused in everyday life as a whole text, rather than one that requires remixing for its pleasure.

Everyone has certain media texts that give them *comfort*. Comfort lives in the space between nostalgia and mastery. For many fans, comfort media reminds them of a time in their lives filled with fond memories of watching a series with a now-deceased family member or friend to remembering the ritual of watching on Saturday nights before going to church on Sunday mornings. As Black *Golden Girls* fans demonstrated, they found comfort in the series because they know *The Golden Girls* inside and out. This is similar to media historian Eleanor Patterson's finding that (mostly white) fans recorded televised wrestling matches on VHS and Beta in order to master the storylines.[7]

In the final analysis, Black fandoms share similarities with other raced fandoms. In that way, Black fandoms are every bit as universal as white fandoms boldly claim to be. However, Black fandoms also depart from the ways other raced fandom groups do fandom, meaning Black fandom is also particular. This universality/particularity dichotomy of Black fandom is rooted in the inherent two-ness of Blackness itself. Black folks see ourselves as ourselves, but also as mainstream culture sees us.[8] In sum, class, clout, canon, and comfort are Black fan practices that are also inherently bifurcated.

Black fandoms are not necessarily, as Black feminist scholar Audre Lorde warned us, attempting to use the master's tools to dismantle the house.[9] Rather, Black folks know that hegemony is like how the late comedian Robin Harris described *Bebe's Kids* (1992, dir. Bruce W. Smith)—it does not die, it multiplies. Thus, Black fandoms attempt to refashion the master's white house into a Black home. As Solange declares in her song "F.U.B.U.," "For us [. . .]. Some shit is a must." Black fandoms are not driven by resistance. They are driven by Black resilience that is elastic and bilingual and allows us to know the master's house at the same time we know our own home. So Black fans enjoy seeing Misty Copeland dance. We find Black joy in heading to the multiplex to see *Black Panther*. Black folks relish the ways *The Wiz* opulently takes a story that was not ours (Baum's *The Wonderful Wizard of Oz*) and crafts it into one that only we can do in that way. Blackness finds a way to make *The Golden Girls*, which was not necessarily meant for us, make sense to us and comfort us. As Black folks, we expend capital to support the kinds of images and media we want to see produced within the media industries. And we use our Black look to try to effect change in media narratives. While we turn our gaze to the mainstream, we also, as Dorothy sings in "Home" from *The Wiz*, "must look inside our hearts to find a world full of love," loving Black media, Black celebrities, and objects that hail our Black selves. We make these objects feel both "like yours, like [ours]" and ultimately "like home."

APPENDIX

Interview Questions

MISTY COPELAND FANDOM QUESTIONNAIRE
1. Tell me what you know about Misty Copeland.
2. How did you first discover Misty Copeland?
3. What is it about Misty Copeland that you love?
4. Why do you describe yourself as a Misty Copeland fan?
5. Are you a fan of ballet generally or just Misty Copeland?
6. Misty Copeland identifies as Black. Does her being mixed race effect your fandom? Why or why not?
7. Have you seen Misty Copeland dance live? Why or why not? If you have seen her dance live, what was the experience like for you?
8. Were you familiar with American Ballet Theatre before becoming a Misty Copeland fan? If so, in what capacity?
9. How do you define a role model? Is Misty Copeland a role model? Why or why not? If she is a role model, for whom is she a role model?
10. Did you have a relationship to dance, ballet and/or the arts before becoming a fan of Misty Copeland? If so, what was that relationship?
11. Do you know the names of any of the following dancers?
    a. Albert Evans (NYCB)
    b. Arthur Mitchell (NYCB, founder of DTH)
    c. Lauren Anderson (Houston Ballet)
    d. Michaela DePrince (Dutch National Ballet)
    e. Virginia Johnson (DTH)
    f. Janet Collins (Ballet Russe de Monte Carlo)
    g. Debra Austin (NYCB, PA Ballet)

BLACK PANTHER INTERVIEWS

1. How often do you go to see a movie in theaters?
2. How do you typically decide which movies to see in theaters versus ones to watch at home?
3. What kind of movies do you typically consume?
4. Do you tend to like Marvel/superhero films?
5. How did you first hear about *Black Panther*?
6. What attracted/excited you to the film?
7. Were you familiar with members of the cast before seeing the film? If so, which ones and how do you know them? Were you familiar with the film's director previously? If so, how so?
8. Did you connect news of the film with the Black Panther Party?
9. What materials did you consumer prior to actually seeing the film? (probe asking about trailers, news/website articles, etc.)
10. When did you see the film? (probe: Opening weekend, the week after its release, later than that?)
11. Why did you choose to see the film when you saw it? (probe: Was it your excitement? Did you want to demonstrate the importance of black audiences to Hollywood?)
12. Who did you see the movie with?
13. Did you see the movie in theaters or did you watch a bootleg copy?
14. Why did you choose to see the movie that way?
15. Did you buy your tickets for the film in advance? If so, why? If not, why not?
16. What expectations did you have about the film prior to seeing it?
17. Did *Black Panther* meet, exceed or fall below your expectations? Why or why not?
18. What did you love about the film?
19. What did you hate about the film?
20. Have you purchased any other material related to the film? (probe: soundtrack, T-shirts, collectibles, etc.)? If so, what kind of material did you purchase? Did you purchase it before or after seeing the film?
21. If you saw the film in theaters, did the theater in which you saw the film do any giveaways? If so, what? If so, did that influence your decision to see the film when you did?

22. Anything else you want to tell me about your experience watching *Black Panther*?

POTLUCK *THE WIZ* QUESTIONS
1. Approximately when did you last watch *The Wiz*?
2. In your life, how many times would you say you've watched *The Wiz*?
3. *The Wiz* came out when we were 2–3 years old; why *The Wiz*?
4. How did you first come across *The Wiz*?
5. What drew you to *The Wiz*?
    a. Is it the movie or the soundtrack or both?
6. What do you like about *The Wiz*?
7. Do you remember how *The Wiz* became our thing?
8. Why do you think *The Wiz* is something we share?
9. What are some memorable moments from our engagement with *The Wiz*?
10. Why *The Wiz* instead of, say, *The Wizard of Oz*? Are they equal in your love?
11. Who watched *The Wiz Live!*? Why/why not? Thoughts on it?
12. Why do you think a nearly 50-year-old movie still endures?
13. Ryan loves *The Wiz*; how did that come about?

BLACK *GOLDEN GIRLS* FANS
1. In what year were you born?
2. Where do you currently live?
3. How do you identify your sexuality?
4. What is your gender identity?
5. What is your relationship status?
6. What is the highest level of education you have completed?
7. In what field do you work?
8. What is your annual household income?
    a. Less than $10,000
    b. More than $10,000 but less than $24,999
    c. More than $25,000 but less than $39,999
    d. More than $40,000 but less than $59,999
    e. More than $60,000 but less than $74,999
    f. More than $75,000 but less than $99,999
    g. More than $100,000

9. How did you find out about this study?
10. Why did you respond?
11. How did you first come to *Golden Girls*?
12. What do you like about *Golden Girls*?
13. Do you remember what shifted you from a *Golden Girls* viewer to a fan?
14. Why do you call yourself a fan versus "just" a viewer?
    a. What separates *Golden Girls* fans from viewers?
15. Do you own any *Golden Girls* merchandise? Have you gone to any *Golden Girls* events? Which one(s)? Why do you own this stuff/ why don't you have any stuff? Do you make anything related to *Golden Girls*?
16. Do you share your fandom with anyone else? Who?
17. Who is your favorite girl?
    a. Why?
18. Do you have a least favorite girl?
    a. Who/why?
19. Do you have a favorite episode?
    a. If so, what is it (or what are they)?
20. Do you have a least favorite episode?
    a. Which one/ones?
21. Do you watch other "friend" coms? (Probe: *Friends, Girlfriends, Living Single, Girls, Sex and the City*)
    a. Are you a viewer or fan of those shows?
    b. How do you distinguish that?
22. There were few Black folks on *Golden Girls*; why do you think it resonates with Black folks like you since it's not about representations of us?
23. *Golden Girls* stopped producing new episodes almost 30 years ago; why do you think it endures?
    a. Is that different from why you think it endures for Black folks?
24. Recently, Hulu announced that it was removing "Mixed Blessings" from the episodes it offered. What do you think about that decision?
25. Which Golden Girl are you?
    a. Why?

ACKNOWLEDGMENTS

While I was writing *Fandom for Us, by Us*, Solange Knowles's song "Almeda" was omnipresent. In the song she expresses her love of "Black skin, Black braids, Black waves, Black days, Black baes, Black things. These are Black-owned things" before reminding us that "Black faith still can't be washed away." And my hope is that *Fandom for Us, by Us* is understood as a love letter to Blackness in the ways Solange expressed her love for Blackness.

Fandom for Us, by Us would not have been possible without the Black people who lent their voices to me to help tell this story. I am forever grateful to each and every one of them for sharing their time and brilliance with me.

I was fortunate to have a lot of Black teachers in the Detroit public school system who taught me with love. Three teachers deserve a special shout-out. My seventh grade English teacher, Ms. Cathy Rowe, not only ignited my love of the written word, but also my love for dance. Her partner in crime, Mr. Jeffrey Nelson, who I first met when he was a substitute teacher at Vetal Elementary School, ignited my creativity through his and Ms. Rowe's production of *The Wiz*. Mr. Dana Payne, my ninth grade English teacher, expanded my vocabulary (and perhaps more importantly, shared my love for Diana Ross).

It truly takes a village to write a book. My village is amazing, and I am grateful to have each and every member of it. Racquel Gates has been, to paraphrase the *Golden Girls* theme song, "a friend and a confidant" as I worked on this book. Thank you for answering every "does this make sense?" text message and finding time to hear me out when I just needed 10 minutes to talk out loud to a smart listener. Thank you to Robin Means Coleman, aka "Dr. Robin," who has been silently (and sometimes not so silently) supporting my work since I met her at a National Communication Association meeting—thanks for the introduction, Khadijah Costley White! Thank you to Jacqueline Bobo, Rebecca

Wanzo, and Kristen Warner for building a body of work on Black audiences and fandoms on which I could build the work I undertake in this book. I am grateful for Andre Brock's friendship, but most of all, for the ways he has modeled how to be a smart, incisive, and Black-as-fuck scholar.

In some ways, *Fandom for Us, by Us* would not have been possible without Jonathan Gray. In his position as editor of the *International Journal of Cultural Studies*, he told me that they infrequently liked work that centered on a single case study. That response led me to think about the ways some of the fandoms I was already examining could be looked at in tandem, and then . . . a book idea emerged. So thank you, Jonathan! Jonathan and Mel Stanfill also read versions of some of the work within *Fandom for Us, by Us*, and for that I remain grateful. Pete Kunze has been a friend and a cheerleader throughout this project. Thank you for reading parts of this book. It's better because of your eyes on it. Thank you for writing with me and helping this book continue to move forward. Nora Patterson is not only one of my best friends in media studies, but she also invited me to give a talk at Auburn University that helped me crystalize the ideas that formed the backbone of *Fandom for Us, by Us*. Henry Jenkins has supported this project from the first time he saw the proposal. Henry, I hope you know how much your encouragement as I worked through this project has meant to me—and the book is stronger because of your insights. I am thankful for the years of friendship with Melissa Click who read this book and gave me feedback in ways that demonstrated her belief in the project and the work it undertakes.

I would be remiss without thanking my family. First up is my Potluck crew—Erica Lott, Cory Lott, Ayanna McConnell, Rhea Norwood, and Roy Rogers. I love you all so hard! And thank you for helping me understand Black canon through our conversations about *The Wiz*. My sister, Yolanda, has supported me through everything—in some ways, she has been more like a mother than a sister, and I am grateful for that love and support. My husband, Tom, has been holding me down for more than two decades. Thank you for all the love, adventures, and mishaps, and I am looking forward to at least two more decades on this amazing ride with you.

Thank you to my father, Al Sr., who supported me no matter what. He took me to my ballet classes and he sat through ballet performances that

I am certain were wholly uninteresting to him. He only completed the ninth grade, but he encouraged me to reach higher and higher through education. I entered grad school because, before he died, we had been discussing whether or not I should do it. My PhD and *Fandom for Us, by Us* are dedicated to him for his love and support for his Black gay son.

Last, but not least, thank you to Blackness. The ingenuity, humor, and duality of Blackness proves that we are, indeed, Black gold. I pour one out for Blackness.

NOTES

INTRODUCTION

1. Christine Acham, *Revolution Televised: Prime Time and the Struggle for Black Power* (Minneapolis: University of Minnesota Press, 2004), 117.
2. Adrien Sebro, *Hustle Economics* (New Brunswick, NJ: Rutgers University Press, 2023), 114–115.
3. Sut Jhally and Justin Lewis, *Enlightened Racism: The Cosby Show, Audiences, and the Myth of the American Dream* (New York: Routledge, 2019).
4. Jean Baudrillard, *Simulacra and Simulation* (Ann Arbor: University of Michigan Press, 1994).
5. Stuart Hall, "Encoding/Decoding in the Television Discourse," in *Channeling Blackness: Studies on Television and Race in America*, ed. Darnell M. Hunt (New York: Oxford University Press, 2005), 46.
6. Clifford Geertz, *The Interpretation of Cultures* (New York: Basic Books, 2000), 26.
7. Julie D'Acci, "Cultural Studies, Television Studies, and the Crisis in the Humanities," in *Television after TV: Essays on a Medium in Transition*, ed. Lynn Spiegel and Jan Olsson (Durham, NC: Duke University Press, 2004), 433.
8. Ibid., 432.
9. Kristen J. Warner, "*Being Mary Jane*: Cultural Specificity," in *How to Watch Television, Second Edition*, ed. Ethan Thompson and Jason Mittell (New York: New York University Press, 2020), 109.
10. Toni Morrison, "Black Studies Center Public Dialogue, Part 2," Portland State University, May 30, 1975, https://pdxscholar.library.pdx.ed. I deliberately differentiate here between racism as a system under which we all live and from which white folks broadly benefit, and racists as individual people enacting racist practices. I am no way suggesting these folks are/were racists, but they are working within and reifying the racism of the academy.
11. Isaac Julien and Kobena Mercer, "De Margin and De Centre," *Screen* 30, no. 1 (1988): 2.
12. Robin R. Means Coleman, ed., *Say It Loud!: African American Audiences, Media and Identity* (New York: Routledge, 2013), 2.
13. Jacqueline Bobo, *Black Women as Cultural Readers* (New York: Columbia University Press, 1995), 209.
14. Rebecca Wanzo, "African American Acafandom and Other Strangers: New Genealogies of Fan Studies," *Transformative Works and Cultures* 20, no. 1 (2015): 1.4.

15 Warner, "Being Mary Jane," 35.
16 Beretta E. Smith-Shomade, *Pimpin 'Ain't Easy: Selling Black Entertainment Television* (New York: Routledge, 2008).
17 Jeffrey A. Brown, *Black Superheroes, Milestone Comics, and Their Fans* (Jackson: University Press of Mississippi, 2009), 2.
18 Alfred L. Martin, Jr., "Fandom While Black: Misty Copeland, Black Panther, Tyler Perry and the Contours of US Black Fandoms," *International Journal of Cultural Studies* 22, no. 6 (2019): 742.
19 Alfred L. Martin, Jr., *The Generic Closet: Black Gayness and the Black-Cast Sitcom* (Bloomington: Indiana University Press, 2021), 12.
20 Patricia Hill Collins, "Learning from the Outsider Within: The Sociological Significance of Black Feminist Thought," *Social Problems* 33, no. 6 (1986): s15.
21 Wanzo, "African American Acafandom," 1.2.
22 Antwuan Sargent, "Arthur Jafa and the Future of Black Cinema," *Interview*, January 11, 2017, www.interviewmagazine.com.
23 Although Twitter is now officially called X, at the time I conducted this research, the platform was still called Twitter, and it will be referenced as such throughout *Fandom for Us, by Us*.
24 Jhally and Lewis, *Enlightened Racism*, 11.
25 Diana Crane, "High Culture Versus Popular Culture Revisited: A Reconceptualization of Recorded Cultures," in *Cultivating Differences: Symbolic Boundaries and the Making of Inequality*, ed. Michéle Lamont and Marcel Fournier (Chicago: University of Chicago Press, 1992), 64.
26 Patricia A. Banks, *Represent: Art and Identity among the Black Upper-Middle Class* (New York: Routledge, 2009), 5.
27 Martin, "Fandom While Black," 741.
28 Nielsen Company, "It's in the Bag: Black Consumers' Path to Purchase," September 12, 2019, 2, www.nielsen.com.
29 Christopher Sieving, *Soul Searching: Black-Themed Cinema from the March on Washington to the Rise of Blaxploitation* (Middletown, CT: Wesleyan University Press, 2011), 24.
30 Frank Segers, "Will 'The Wiz' Ease on Down the Road to Box-Office Ahs?," *Variety*, October 12, 1978, 2.

CHAPTER 1. CLASS

1 Misty Copeland, *Life in Motion: An Unlikely Ballerina* (New York: Touchstone Books, 2014), 102–103.
2 Ibid., 112.
3 Cassi Pittman Claytor, *Black Privilege: Modern Middle-Class Blacks with Credentials and Cash to Spend* (Stanford, CA: Stanford University Press, 2020, 1).
4 Patricia A. Banks, *Represent: Art and Identity among the Black Upper-Middle Class* (New York: Routledge, 2009), 5.

5   Crystal M. Fleming and Lorraine E. Roses, "Black Cultural Capitalists: African-American Elites and the Organization of the Arts in Early Twentieth Century Boston," *Poetics* 35, no. 6 (2007): 376.
6   Alfred L. Martin, Jr., "Why All the Hate?: Four Black Women's Anti-Fandom and Tyler Perry," in *Anti-Fandom: Dislike and Hate in the Digital Age*, ed. Melissa A. Click (New York: New York University Press, 2019), 175.
7   Alfred L. Martin, Jr., "Fandom While Black: Misty Copeland, *Black Panther*, Tyler Perry and the Contours of US Black Fandoms," *International Journal of Cultural Studies* 22, no. 6 (2019): 737–753.
8   Pierre Bourdieu, *Distinction* (New York: Routledge, 1984), 56.
9   American Ballet Theatre, "United States Congress Honors American Ballet Theatre: Recognized for 65 Years of Service as 'America's National Ballet Company,'" ABT.org, May 25, 2006, www.abt.org.
10 Chris Rojek, *Celebrity* (London: Reaktion Books, 2004), 35.
11 Laura Bleiberg, "Misty Copeland, Calvin Royal III and the Rarity of a Black Couple Dancing Lead Roles," *Los Angeles Times*, January 15, 2019, www.latimes.com.
12 BET.com, "Famous vs. Black Famous, Continued," December 2, 2013, www.bet.com.
13 "Prince Was a Queen-Maker," Pitchfork, April 20, 2017, https://pitchfork.com.
14 Jonathan Gray, *Show Sold Separately* (New York: New York University Press, 2010), 3.
15 Nicole Fleetwood, *Troubling Vision: Performance, Visuality, and Blackness* (Chicago, University of Chicago Press, 2011), 29.
16 CreatedByKisha [@CreatedByKisha], "Ainsley Loves Ballet," Instagram, February 11, 2021, https://www.instagram.com/p/CLJz8TalFJG.
17 Michel Foucault, *Discipline and Punish: The Birth of the Prison* (New York: Random House, 1977), 27.
18 Bourdieu, *Distinction*, 49.
19 Ibid.
20 As of June 2023, there are seven Black ballet dancers on ABT's roster: Copeland and Royal are principal dancers. Gabe Stone Shayer is a soloist; he joined the company in 2012 and was promoted to soloist in 2020—incidentally, the same year Royal was promoted to principal. Erica Lall, Courtney Lavine, Melvin Lavowi, and Aleisha Walker are members of ABTs corps de ballet.
21 Fleming and Roses, "Black Cultural Capitalists," 369.
22 Bourdieu, *Distinction*, 40.
23 Ibid., 14.
24 Martin, "Fandom While Black," 746.
25 *Time* Staff, "Read the Full Transcript of *Time*'s Conversation with President Obama and Misty Copeland," *Time*, March 14, 2016, https://time.com.
26 Copeland, *Life in Motion*, 272, 313.
27 Fleetwood, *Troubling Vision*, 109.
28 C. Lee Harrington, Denise D. Bielby, and Anthony R. Bardo, "Life Course Transitions and the Future of Fandom," *International Journal of Cultural Studies* 14, no. 6 (2011): 583.

29 Andrea Shaw, "The Other Side of the Looking Glass: The Marginalization of Fatness and Blackness in the Construction of Gender Identity," *Social Semiotics* 15, no. 2 (2005): 146.
30 *Time* staff, "Read the Full Transcript."
31 Samantha N. Sheppard, *Sporting Blackness: Race, Embodiment, and Critical Muscle Memory on Screen* (Berkeley: University of California Press, 2020), 139.
32 Matt Hills, "Returning to 'Becoming-a-Fan' Stories: Theorising Transformational Objects and the Emergence/Extension of Fandom," in *The Ashgate Research Companion to Fan Cultures*, ed. Linda Duits, Koos Zwaan, and Stun Reunders (London: Routledge, 2016), 10.
33 bell hooks, *Black Looks: Race and Representation* (Boston: South End Press, 1992), 120.
34 Herman Gray, *Cultural Moves: African Americans and the Politics of Representation* (Berkeley: University of California Press, 2005), 186.
35 John Fiske, *Media Matters: Race and Gender in U.S. Politics* (Minneapolis: University of Minnesota Press, 1996), 69.
36 The website MoBBallet.org curates a list of Black ballet dancers: https://mobballet.org/index.php/impact.
37 Henry Jenkins, Sam Ford, and Joshua Green, *Spreadable Media: Creating Value and Meaning in a Networked World* (New York: New York University Press, 2018).

CHAPTER 2. CLOUT

1 The Tonight Show Starring Jimmy Fallon channel, "Chadwick Boseman Surprises Black Panther Fans While They Thank Him," YouTube.com, February 28, 2018, https://www.youtube.com/watch?v=expKmfdoo28&ab_channel=TheTonightShowStarringJimmyFallon.
2 Kristen Warner, "In the Time of Plastic Representation," *Film Quarterly* 71, no. 2 (2017): 32–37.
3 Allyson Field, *Uplift Cinema: The Emergence of African American Film and the Possibility of Black Modernity* (Durham, NC: Duke University Press, 2015), 3.
4 Beschara Karam and Mark Kirby-Hirst, "Guest Editorial for Themed Section *Black Panther* and Afrofuturism: Theoretical Discourse and Review," *Image & Text* 33 (2019): 5–6.
5 Stuart Hall, "Encoding/Decoding in the Television Discourse," in *Channeling Blackness: Studies on Television and Race in America*, ed. Darnell M. Hunt (New York: Oxford University Press, 2005), 46.
6 Ellen Seiter, *Sold Separately: Children and Parents in Consumer Culture* (New Brunswick, NJ: Rutgers University Press, 1993), 6.
7 Rebecca Wanzo, "African American Acafandom and Other Strangers: New Genealogies of Fan Studies," *Transformative Works and Cultures* 20, no. 1 (2015): 2.15.
8 bell hooks, *Black Looks: Race and Representation* (Boston: South End Press, 1992), 116.

9 Alfred L. Martin, Jr., "Fandom While Black: Misty Copeland, *Black Panther*, Tyler Perry, and the Contours of US Black Fandoms," *International Journal of Cultural Studies* 22, no. 6 (2019): 741.
10 Beretta Smith Shomade, *Pimpin' Ain't Easy: Selling Black Entertainment Television* (New York: Routlege, 2007), 28.
11 Sameer Rao, "*Girls Trip* Earns Estimated $30+ Million in Opening Weekend," Colorlines, July 24, 2017, https://colorlines.com.
12 Spencer Baculi, "Viola Davis Says That Audiences Who Don't See 'The Woman King' Are 'Supporting the Narrative That Black Women Cannot Lead the Box Office Globally,'" Bounding into Comics, September 14, 2022, https://bounding intocomics.com.
13 Robert E. Weems, *Desegregating the Dollar: African American Consumerism in the Twentieth Century* (New York: New York University Press, 1998), 2–3.
14 Steven D. Classes, *Watching Jim Crow: The Struggles over Mississippi TV, 1955–1969* (Durham, NC: Duke University Press, 2004), 53.
15 Bambi L. Haggins, "Why 'Beulah' and 'Andy' Still Play Today: Minstrelsy in the New Millennium," *Emergences: Journal for the Study of Media & Composite Cultures* 11, no. 2 (2001): 249–267.
16 Billy Rowe, "'The Wiz'—A $30 Million Gamble," *Call and Post*, November 11, 1978, 6A.
17 Andy Bowers, "First Weekend Club," National Public Radio, December 23, 1998, www.npr.org.
18 Sarah Banet Weiser, *Kids Rule!: Nickelodeon and Consumer Citizenship* (Durham, NC: Duke University Press, 2007), 9.
19 Arlene Davila, *Latinos Inc.: The Marketing and Making of a People* (Berkeley: University of California Press, 2012).
20 Jen Yamato, "Chadwick Boseman Signed for 5 Films as Black Panther, Captain Marvel Bring Diversity to Superhero Slate," *Deadline*, October 28, 2014, https://deadline.com.
21 Justin Wyatt, *High Concept: Movies and Marketing in Hollywood* (Austin: University of Texas Press, 1994), 94.
22 Alfred L. Martin, Jr., "Surplus Blackness," *Flow Journal*, April 27, 2021, www.flow journal.org.
23 Martin, "Fandom While Black," 741.
24 Kristen J. Warner, "*Being Mary Jane*: Cultural Specificity," in *How to Watch Television, Second Edition*, ed. Ethan Thompson and Jason Mittell (New York: New York University Press, 2020), 109.
25 Maryann Eringha, *The Hollywood Jim Crow: The Racial Politics of the Movie Industry* (New York: New York University Press, 2019), 52.
26 Tom Huddleston, Jr., "An Especially Diverse Audience Lifted 'Black Panther' to Record Box Office Heights," *Fortune*, February 21, 2018, https://fortune.com.
27 Racquel J. Gates, *Double Negative: The Black Image and Popular Culture* (Durham, NC: Duke University Press, 2018), 58.

28 Alfred L. Martin, Jr., "Blackbusting Hollywood: Racialized Media Reception, Failure, and The Wiz as Black Blockbuster," *JCMS: Journal of Cinema and Media Studies* 60, no. 2 (2021): 57.
29 Tim Havens, *Black Television Travels: African American Media Across the Globe* (New York: New York University Press, 2013), 78.
30 Kara Keeling, *Queer Times, Black Futures* (New York: New York University Press, 2019), 4.
31 "For the Culture," Urban Dictionary, www.urbandictionary.com.
32 hooks, *Black Looks*, 116.
33 Elana Levine and Michael Newman, *Legitimating Television: Media Convergence and Cultural Status* (New York: Routledge, 2012), 99.
34 hooks, *Black Looks*, 21.
35 Timothy Havens and Amanda Lotz, *Understanding Media Industries* (New York: Oxford University Press, 2019).
36 Charles H. Cooley, *Human Nature and the Social Order* (New York: Charles Scribner's Sons, 2006).
37 FrederickJoseph.com, homepage, retrieved February 23, 2023, https://frederickjoseph.com.
38 Kodwo Eshun, "Further Considerations of Afrofuturism," *CR: The New Centennial Review* 3, no. 2 (2003): 298.
39 Geena Davis Institute on Gender in Media, https://seejane.org, retrieved May 2, 2023.
40 Ibid.
41 Alfred L. Martin Jr., "The Queer Business of Casting Gay Characters on US Television," *Communication Culture & Critique* 11, no. 2 (2018): 290.

CHAPTER 3. CANON

1 Christopher Sieving, *Soul Searching: Black-Themed Cinema from the March on Washington to the Rise of Blaxploitation* (Middletown, CT: Wesleyan University Press, 2011), 24.
2 Raizel Liebler and Keidra Chaney, "Canon vs . Fanon: Folksonomies of Fan Culture," paper for presentation at Media in Transition 5: Creativity, Ownership and Collaboration in the Digital Age (2007): 1. www.academia.edu.
3 Patricia Hill Collins, "Learning from the Outsider Within: The Sociological Significance of Black Feminist Thought," *Social Problems* 33, no. 6 (1986): s14.
4 Carolyn Ellis, Tony E. Adams, and Arthur P. Bochner, "Autoethnography: An Overview," *Historical Social Research*, 36, no. 4 (2011): 273.
5 Jacqueline Bobo, *Black Women as Cultural Readers* (New York: Columbia University Press, 1995), 22.
6 Sarah Florini, "Enclaving and Cultural Resonance in Black 'Game of Thrones' Fandom," *Transformative Works and Cultures* 29 (2019): 1.4.
7 Stanley E. Fish, "Interpreting the 'Variorum,'" *Critical Inquiry* 2, no. 3 (1976): 483.

8 Janet Staiger, "The Politics of Film Canons," *Cinema Journal* (1985): 4.
9 Lisa Alexander, *Expanding the Black Film Canon: Race and Genre across Six Decades* (Lawrence: University of Kansas Press, 2019), 6.
10 Stuart Hall, "What Is This 'Black' in Black Popular Culture," *Social Justice* 20, no. 1/2 (1993): 107–108.
11 Ahuvia Kahane, "Fan Fiction, Early Greece, and the Historicity of Canon," *Transformative Works and Cultures* 21 (2016): 1.3.
12 Sarah Benyahia and Claire Mortimer, *Doing Film Studies: A Subject Guide for Studies* (New York: Routledge, 2013), 36.
13 Ibid.
14 Lewis R. Gordon, "Black Aesthetics, Black Value," *Public Culture* 30, no. 1 (2018): 19–34; 30.
15 Alfred L. Martin, Jr., "Blackbusting Hollywood: Racialized Media Reception, Failure, and *The Wiz* as Black Blockbuster," *JCMS: Journal of Cinema and Media Studies* 60, no. 2 (2021): 60.
16 Stuart Hall, "Encoding/Decoding in the Television Discourse," in *Channeling Blackness: Studies on Television and Race in America*, ed. Darnell M. Hunt (New York: Oxford University Press, 2005).
17 Thomas Cripps, *Black Film as Genre* (Bloomington: Indiana University Press, 1979), 3.
18 Ernest Mathijs and Xavier Mendik, "Editorial Introduction: What Is Cult Film?," in *The Cult Film Reader* (New York: Open University Press, 2008), 11.
19 Archer Winsten, "Sets Walk Away with 'The Wiz,'" *New York Post*, October 24, 1978, 69.
20 For a fuller accounting of white reviews of *The Wiz*, see Martin, "Blackbusting Hollywood."
21 Alamo Drafthouse, *The Wiz*, https://drafthouse.com.
22 Mathijs and Mendik, "Editorial Introduction," 11.
23 Martin, "Blackbusting Hollywood," 69.
24 Marie Moore, "Gee Wiz!," *New York Amsterdam News*, November 4, 1978, D10.
25 "The Yellow Brick Road Is Paved with Gold!," *Variety*, November 1, 1978, 8–9.
26 Paul C. Taylor, *Black Is Beautiful: A Philosophy of Black Aesthetics* (Malden, MA: Wiley Blackwell, 2016), 23–24.
27 Henry Jenkins, *Textual Poachers: Television Fans and Participatory Culture* (New York: Routledge, 2012).
28 Original Broadway Cast, "The Feeling That We Have," track 3 on *The Wiz* (original soundtrack), Motown Records, 1978.
29 Ibid.
30 Racquel Gates, "Activating the Negative Image," *Television & New Media* 16, no. 7 (2015): 623.
31 Tyrone S. Palmer, "'What Feels More than Feeling?': Theorizing the Unthinkability of Black Affect," *Critical Ethnic Studies* 3, no. 2 (2017): 51.

32 Lisa M. Corrigan, *Black Feelings: Race and Affect in the Long Sixties* (Jackson: University Press of Mississippi, 2020), xxi.
33 Susanna Paasonen, *Carnal Resonance: Affect and Online Pornography* (Cambridge, MA: MIT Press, 2024), 16.
34 "Flow," Urban Dictionary, www.urbandictionary.com.
35 Neda Yodovich, "Like Father, Like Daughter: The Intergenerational Passing of *Doctor Who* and *Star Wars* Fandom in the Familial Context," in *Fandom, The Next Generation*, ed. Bridget Kies and Megan Connor (Iowa City: University of Iowa Press, 2022), 66.
36 Alfred L. Martin, Jr., "Fandom While Black: Misty Copeland, Black Panther, Tyler Perry and the Contours of US Black Fandoms," *International Journal of Cultural Studies* 22, no. 6 (2019): 741.
37 Taylor Cole Miller, "Re witched: Retextuality and the Queering of *Bewitched*," *Camera Obscura* 36, no. 3 (2021): 1–31.
38 Splinters Apprentice, "Connections between RWT and *The Wiz*," Reddit, 2023, https://www.reddit.com/r/beyonce/comments/16eolfo/connections_between_rwt_and_the_wiz.
39 Hall, "Encoding/Decoding."
40 Alfred L. Martin, Jr., "Why All the Hate?: Four Black Women's Anti-fandom and Tyler Perry," in *Anti-Fandom: Dislike and Hate in the Digital Age*, ed. Melissa A. Click (New York: New York University Press, 2019), 166.
41 Kristen Warner, "The Pleasure Principle of *Magic Mike XXL*: Sonic Visibility toward Female Audiences," *Communication Culture & Critique* 12, no. 2 (2019): 231.
42 Paul Booth and Peter Kelly, "The Changing Faces of *Doctor Who* Fandom: New Fans, New Technologies, Old Practices?," *Participations* 10, no. 1 (May 2013): 67.
43 Ibid.
44 Andre Cavalcante, "Breaking into Transgender Life: Transgender Audiences' Experiences with 'First of Its Kind' Visibility in Popular Media," *Communication, Culture, and Critique* 10 (2017): 539.
45 Simon Critchley, *On Humor* (New York: Routledge, 2002), 68–69.
46 Dick Hebdige, "Subculture," in *Popular Culture: A Reader*, ed. Raiford Guins and Omayra Zaragoza Cruz (Los Angeles: Sage Publications, 2005), 359.
47 Annette Kuhn, "'That Day Did Last Me All My Life': Cinema Memory and Enduring Fandom," in *Identifying Hollywood's Audiences: Cultural Identity and the Movies*, ed. Melvyn Stokes and Richard Maltby (London: British Film Institute, 1999), 136.
48 Bobo, *Black Women as Cultural Readers*.
49 Alfred L. Martin, Jr., "Finding the Funny: Recentering the *Comedy* in Black Comedy," in *Rolling: Blackness and Mediated Comedy*, ed. Alfred L. Martin, Jr. (Bloomington: Indiana University Press, 2024), 2.
50 Barbara Klinger, *Beyond the Multiplex: Cinema, New Technologies, and the Home* (Berkeley: University of California Press, 2006), 182.

CHAPTER 4. COMFORT

1 Barbara Klinger, *Beyond the Multiplex: Cinema, New Technologies, and the Home* (Berkeley: University of California Press, 2006), 151.
2 Susanna Paasonen, *Carnal Resonance: Affect and Online Pornography* (Cambridge, MA: MIT Press, 2011), 16.
3 Kristen Warner, "The Pleasure Principle of *Magic Mike XXL*: Sonic Visibility toward Female Audiences," *Communication, Culture & Critique* 12, no. 2 (2019): 235.
4 Rebecca Williams, *Post-object Fandom: Television, Identity and Self-Narrative* (London: Bloomsbury, 2015), 16.
5 Racquel Gates, "Activating the Negative Image," *Television and New Media* 16, no. 7 (2015): 624.
6 Klinger, *Beyond the Multiplex*, 155.
7 Caetlin Benson Allot, "In Praise of Escapism," *Film Quarterly* 74, no. 1 (Fall 2020): 75.
8 Derek Kompare, *Rerun Nation: How Repeats Invented American Television* (New York: Routledge, 2005), 69.
9 John Koblin, "Lockdown TV: Netflix Dominates, News Surges and Bea Arthur Is Still Golden," *New York Times*, April 30, 2020, www.nytimes.com.
10 Kathryn VanArendonk, "We're Living in an Era of Peak Comfort TV," Vulture, July 8, 2020, www.vulture.com.
11 Charlotte E. Howell and Joyce B. Howell, "Happy Trees in a Black Box: *The Joy of Painting with Bob Ross*' Elevated Escapism as Comfort TV," *Journal of Cinema and Media Studies*, forthcoming.
12 Klinger, *Beyond the Multiplex*, 154.
13 Alfred L. Martin, Jr., "Re-watching Omar: *Moesha*, Black Gayness and Shifting Media Reception," *Flow*, February 1, 2021, www.flowjournal.org.
14 Eleanor Patterson, "The Golden Girls Live: Residual Television Texts, Participatory Culture, and Queering TV Heritage through Drag," *Feminist Media Studies* 16, no. 5 (2016): 838–851; Alexander Doty, *Making Things Perfectly Queer: Interpreting Mass Culture* (Minneapolis: University of Minnesota Press, 1993), 6.
15 Finally Aaron, "The Golden Girls Gospel Remix (Full Song)," YouTube.com, February 11, 2016, https://www.youtube.com/watch?v=mWD_VPiMlso&ab_channel=FinallyAaron.
16 Bridget McDaniel, "The Black Golden Girls," YouTube.com, May 17, 2019, https://www.youtube.com/watch?v=vnCvO_Egfuc&ab_channel=BridgetMcDaniel.
17 Sarah Florini, "Enclaving and Cultural Resonance in Black *Game of Thrones* Fandom," *Transformative Works and Cultures* 29, no. 1 (2019): 2.1.
18 Henry Jenkins, *Textual Poachers: Television Fans and Participatory Culture* (New York: Routledge, 2012).
19 First We Feast, "Gabrielle Union Impersonates DMX While Eating Spicy Wings | Hot Ones," YouTube.com, November 2, 2017, https://www.youtube.com/watch?v=twjTkBN3Q9A&ab_channel=FirstWeFeast.

20 Rachel Yang, "Tracee Ellis Ross, Regina King, and More Will Do Their Own *Golden Girls* Rendition for Zoom Special," *Entertainment Weekly*, September 7, 2020, https://ew.com.
21 Trina G, Twitter post, September 8, 2020, 8:45 p.m., https://twitter.com/dharma69/status/1303509682418458624.
22 Warner, "Pleasure Principle of *Magic Mike XXL*," 243.
23 Jamal's Keeper, Twitter post, September 8, 2020, 9:08 p.m., https://twitter.com/TheRastaEmpress/status/1303515711906734085.
24 Raymond Williams, *Marxism and Literature* (New York: Oxford University Press, 1977), 132.
25 Janet Staiger, *Blockbuster TV: Must-See Sitcoms of the Network Era* (New York: New York University Press, 2000).
26 Lee Margulies, "NBC Starts Fast in Ratings Race," *Los Angeles Times*, September 18, 1985, www.latimes.com, and Lee Margulies, "TV Ratings: A Golden Week for NBC," *Los Angeles Times*, May 13, 1992, www.latimes.com.
27 John Fiske, *Understanding Popular Culture*, 2nd ed. (New York: Routledge, 2010).
28 Marlon B. Ross, "Camping the Dirty Dozens: The Queer Resources of Black Nationalist Invective," *Callaloo* 23, no. 1 (Winter 2000): 291.
29 Lynn Spigel, *Make Room for TV: Television and the Family Ideal in Postwar America* (Chicago: University of Chicago Press, 1992).
30 Jonathan Gray, *Watching with The Simpsons: Television, Parody, and Intertextuality* (New York: Routledge, 2006), 49.
31 Paasonen, *Carnal Resonance*, 16.
32 Klinger, *Beyond the Multiplex*, 57.
33 Williams, *Marxism and Literature*, 132.
34 See Suzanne Scott, *Fake Geek Girls: Fandom, Gender, and the Convergence Culture Industry* (New York: New York University Press, 2019), and Rukmini Pande, *Squee from the Margins: Fandom and Race* (Iowa City: University of Iowa Press, 2018).

CONCLUSION

1 Amy Howe, "Supreme Court Strikes Down Affirmative Action Programs in College Admissions," *SCOTUS Blog*, June 29, 2023, www.scotusblog.com.
2 Herman Gray, "Subject (ed) to Recognition," *American Quarterly* 65, no. 4 (2013): 781.
3 Jonathan Gray, Cornel Sandvoss, and C. Lee Harrington, eds., *Fandom: Identities and Communities in a Mediated World* (New York: New York University Press, 2017), 4.
4 Matt Marshall, "Misty Copeland Reflects on the 'Generational Trauma' Felt by Black Ballet Dancers," CNN.com, March 24, 2024, www.cnn.com.
5 Henry Jenkins, "Afterword: The Future of Fandom," in *Fandom: Identities and Communities in a Mediated World*, ed. Jonathan Gray, Cornel Sandvoss, and C. Lee Harrington (New York: New York University Press, 2017), 359–360.

6 Victoria M. Gonzalez, "Swan Queen, Shipping, and Boundary Regulation in Fandom," *Transformative Works and Cultures* 22, no. 1 (2016): n.p.
7 Eleanor Patterson, *Bootlegging the Airwaves: Alternative Histories of Radio and Television Distribution* (Urbana: University of Illinois Press, 2024).
8 William Edward Burghardt Du Bois, *The Souls of Black Folk* (New York: Oxford University Press, 2008).
9 Audre Lorde, *The Master's Tools Will Never Dismantle the Master's House* (London: Penguin UK, 2018).

INDEX

Abrera, Stella, 27
Addison, Katlyn, 54
aesthetics, 115–6
affect, 116–8, 135, 163
African American Vernacular English (AAVE), 12
Ailey, Alvin, 40
Alexander, Lisa, 102–3
Allot, Caetlin Benson, 133
American Ballet Theater (ABT), 23, 24, 27, 28, 38–44, 48, 54, 162
Anderson, Lauren, 43
Austin, Debra, 43, 54

Baudrillard, Jean, 4
Black culture, 57–94
Black fandom, 5–7, 8–11, 38–44, 124–5, 161–7
Black futurity, 79–84
Black Panther, 10, 12, 16–17, 44, 57–94, 162–3; importance to fans, 66–68. *See also* clout
Black resonance, 145–8
Black style, 64–68
Blackish, 64–66
Blackness, intergenerational, 119–21
Bobo, Jacqueline, 8, 49, 127
Brock-Akil, Mara, 7

canon, 3, 4, 14–19, 95–126, 163, 165; definition of, 99–100; theory of, 102; as Black fan practice, 103, 109. *See also The Wiz*
celebrity, production of, 26–29
Civil Rights Movement, 62, 107, 161

class (socioeconomic) 3, 4, 14–19, 23–56; Americanness of, 54–55. *See also* Copeland, Misty
Clayton, Cassi Pittman, 22–23
clout, 3, 4, 14–19, 57–94, 163; definition of, 58–9; looking glass of, 84–90. *See also Black Panther*
Coleman, Robin Means, 8
Collins, Janet, 43
comfort, 3, 4, 14–19, 127–60, 163–4, 166–7. *See also The Golden Girls*
Copeland, Misty, 10, 14–15, 23–56, 162, 164–5; as role model, 44–54; fans discovering, 29–30; visibility of, 48–50. *See also* class (socioeconomic)
Corrigan, Lisa, 110

Dance Theater of Harlem (DTH), 23–4, 40, 43
distinction, 23–56

familiarity, 155–9
Fentroy, Chrystyn, 54
Fish, Stanley, 100
Florini, Sarah, 146
Fogo, Nikisha, 54

Gates, Racquel, 109, 133
Geertz, Clifford, 5
Gray, Herman, 53
Gray, Jonathan, 164
The Golden Girls, 10, 12, 18–19, 127–60, 163–4, 166–7; *The Black Golden Girls*, 146–8. *See also* comfort
Good Times, 3–4

189

Haggins, Bambi, 62
Harrington, C. Lee, 164
hooks, bell, 59–60

interpretative communities, 95–126

Jackson, Michael, 2, 3–4
Jenkins, Henry, 165
Johnson, Virginia, 43

Keys, Alicia, 95, 97
Klinger, Barbara, 133–4
Kompare, Derek, 134

Mearns, Sara, 27
methodology, 12–14, 129
Miller, Taylor Cole, 112–3
Monja, Claudia, 54
must-see Blackness, 60–61, 67–68, 81–81, 120, 163; definition of, 16

openness, 149–51

potluck, 95–126
Prince, 26, 28

representation, 3–5, 79–84; "negative" representation, 63
resonance, 127–60; politics of, 127–8
respectability politics, 23–24
retextualization, 112–4, 121–4
Rowe, Billy, 62

Sandvoss, Cornell, 164
School Daze, 95
Smith Shomade, Beretta, 8, 9, 60
Solange, 7–8, 167
Swan Lake, 22

visibility, politics of, 160

Wanzo, Rebecca, 18, 20
Warner, Kristen, 128
Weiser, Sarah Banet, 63
Wilkinson, Raven, 43
Williams, Rebecca, 128
The Wiz, 10, 17–18, 95–126, 163; as "bad," 106; fandom of, 110–1; white reviews of, 106. *See also* canon

Yodovich, Neta, 111

ABOUT THE AUTHOR

ALFRED L. MARTIN, JR., is Chair and Associate Professor in the Department of Cinematic Arts at University of Miami. He is author of *The Generic Closet: Black Gayness and the Black-Cast Sitcom*, editor of *Rolling: Blackness and Mediated Comedy*, and co-editor of *The Golden Girls: Essays from the Lanai*.

www.ingramcontent.com/pod-product-compliance
Lightning Source LLC
Jackson TN
JSHW022314140625
86154JS00004B/7